Living Within
—— the ——
Confinements
of Lupus

DEBBIE HOLLINS

WESTBOW
P R E S S®
A DIVISION OF THOMAS NELSON
& ZONDERVAN

WestBow Press books may be ordered through booksellers or by contacting:

WestBow Press
A Division of Thomas Nelson & Zondervan
1663 Liberty Drive
Bloomington, IN 47403
www.westbowpress.com
844-714-3454

ISBN: 978-1-6642-4457-3 (sc)
ISBN: 978-1-6642-4459-7 (hc)
ISBN: 978-1-6642-4458-0 (e)

Library of Congress Control Number: 2021918581

Print information available on the last page.

WestBow Press rev. date: 11/15/2021

Jehovah Rapha (The Lord that Heals) Exodus 15:26

Contents

Dedication

This book is dedicated to everyone who is Living
Within the Confinements of Lupus.

Acknowledgments

I honor the Holy Spirit for teaching me and showing me the way out of Lupus and providing me wisdom on writing this book.

Special thanks to my husband Robert for supporting and believing in me. For his love and patience, my prayer partner.

My mother, Eva Morrow, for her love and understanding, always believed in me. She always told me that my hands are blessed by God.

To my family, thanks for all the love and support and prayers.

To my church family, thank you for your love, support, prayers, strength, and wisdom through the most challenging time of Lupus.

Introduction

The purpose of Living Within the Confinements of Lupus provides an understanding that there's a way to escape. You don't have to be held hostage to your problem. Lupus comes to rob you from living your life in fullness. Living within definitely overwhelms one life. You are desperately trying to figure everything out. But how can you, when the ability to think and focus is not apparent? Some days are good, and some days are bad, and you find yourself trapped in the midst of them looking for someone to understand you. Lupus, at times, makes you feel like a stranger in your body and to your loved ones and friends. Finding yourself pulled in different places, not knowing how you readily enter in that place. In that place, you become emotionally and lonely. You are living in the unknown, the uncertainty, and the place of isolation. You are trying to make good choices and good sound decisions, but you are in a fog, the inward cries from within. The day you feel like the doctor gave you a death sentence. Hope is just hope; despair is there. Lock into your own little world of unknown, invisible friends.

In 1989 when a doctor diagnosed me with SLE, known as Systemic Lupus Erythematosus. My life changed; it was terrible and, yes frightening, it was hard to explain at times. It's now 2021, isn't God good and faithful to His Word. God wants me to tell you; you can make it through. He loves you and wants you healed, whole, and delivered from your bondage that comes to hold you hostage against your will.

I traveled this journey for a reason and recognize there was a bigger and better reason than I could have imagined. Let me inspire you to switch partners to get on the right side, where there is love, joy, peace, hope, faith, and endurance. In this book, I shared my Lupus story, my emotional overdrive, how my morning didn't belong to me anymore, and how I became desperately waiting. I also shared doctor's visits, even the enemy in disguise trying to inflict my body. Also shared the unfolding of the unknown, the hidden secret I kept and shared later on. I was trying to say goodbye. I prepared truths, knowledge, meditation, and other things to help you. All you have to do is reach out, and this book will draw you. One important thing to walk your way through your healing is to have a relationship with God. Stay before him, learn of him. What I like most of all, the Holy Spirit will teach you many things God wants you to know. Let this book guide you through your journey. Most of all, God loves you and wants you healed, whole, and delivered.

Stories

My Emotional Overdrive

Throughout my emotional overdrive, I was overwhelmed with days filled with mixed emotions. These emotions gave me the right to say whatever was on my mind. It was never my intention to harm anyone, especially God. Those emotions were driving me, pulling me in the wrong direction. There was no way of seeing things correctly. How could I? Wounded deep within my soul? This rage had a grip on me. Hear me. I was so enraged that I was furious at God. There was no reasoning, I believed God did this horrible, terrible, outrageous, unbelievable thing. My heart was saying, how could God do this to me? Every time I thought about God doing this, the more my anger grew. It shifts to an unpleasant attitude. Yes, it got the best of me. My words turned against God, and I found myself not caring anymore. How could God let me down like this? What made God think this would be OK? I kept thinking, God has some kind of nerve here. Didn't he know this was going to destroy me? What was He thinking? I couldn't figure this out. What was the purpose, the reason God would treat me like this? I was already hurting, but to add more on me wasn't fair, at all. My mind was racing, I needed to figure this out. Maybe he would step in, just waiting for me, or maybe I had done something but I don't know what it was. My heart knew better, but my mind refused to let me see it differently. I thought God would try to put an end to it, then all of a sudden, I realized it wasn't going to stop. I believe God had made his final decision in this matter.

The rage grew, and no matter how hard I tried, the feeling refused to turn me loose. Lord, You know I tried not to take it to that level of being mean. My emotions were out of control. There was no turning back; words released out of my mouth were hurtful. At this point, I could no longer hold anything in, so I let it all out. My tone with God was harsh. I had to give him a piece of my mind. I tried my best not to be hateful, but the anger grew. I could feel the anger building up within me; it was too strong. I heard a voice saying, no, don't you do that. I opened up the bathroom door, and let it all go. I knew who the voice was and let go anyhow. About this time, I was completely fed up with God. He'd done it, he'd caused it, and now he was going to listen to me. How could you do me like this, betray me like this? What have I done in my life to deserve this? What have I ever done, unto you Lord? I thought you loved me? There is no kind of love here. No Lord! You don't deserve my praise; you are not my Father anymore. There is no trust here when you know how I feel and view things. Why would you do this? Why would you wait for me to fall in love with you and then this? I thought I finally had what I needed; you took it away, Lord. I've given you my heart and soul, and this is how you repay me. This is how you treat me! This is how you value; no, God, you tell me how I'm supposed to go through this ordeal. "You have truly hurt my heart, do you understand? I can't trust you or rely on you anymore. What have you done to me? I have nothing anymore! I am dying, Lord! Do you care? Do you realize I won't be here for my son?"

Suddenly, I heard, "I gave up my son." In my mind, I said, "it's not about you, it's about me." Yet somehow my heart did go out to God because of what he'd said. Suddenly, I went back and said, "My son, God. It's not fair, at all. I will not see him grow up, see him march across the stage to graduate, or see his family. You tell me, What do I have to live for now? What? You know what, Lord, you are big and bad! You come on now! Come on and take me now! Come on off your throne, and take me, here I am, Lord! Come on! You come on; you're the all-powerful and all-knowing God; you're going to take me out anyway. Come on here from your throne! I don't fear you, and I am not scared of you. Do you think I want to live like this? I am not playing; come on here. There is no hope; all I have left is pain and sorrow, no love, no joy, and certainly no forgiveness. I am sick of you. I am sick and tired of you. You know what, God, you can leave me alone. I don't want you, nor do I need you. You get out of my life. Get out of my life now! You go! After what you've done, I feel like you've turned your back on me. You caused this terrible ordeal, you didn't even stop it from happening. You could have blinked an eye, one eye, Lord-, but you didn't! You stood by and watched!No father Lord, in their right mind would have ever done their child as you have done me. No father Lord, but you did. So, guess what? Love doesn't live here anymore."

How could I accept what I didn't appreciate? In my mind and heart, God did me wrong. He broke my heart! I was justified in my action toward God. Keep in mind; when I gave God a piece of my mind, it didn't happen at this moment. It was after the unfolding of the unknown story. God wanted you to see this part of the story now!

My Morning Doesn't
Belong to Me Anymore

P eople say your day is what you make of it. Tell me how when living is not easy to do now? Days filled with uncertainty, the pathway is dim and rocky, and I grasp for every opportunity and possibility coming my way. I still have hope, still trust in God, faithfully going to church, and doing everything to hold on. One thing I never counted on was this thing controlling me and creeping up on me without any notice. It doesn't need permission to move to violate me, to trespass on my body. I'm so within myself, don't know how to tell anyone, and don't know how they will respond. The everyday reality wasn't the same, but O' those dreadful mornings dreaded them all. Tell me how a person can lay down one way and get up another way. Being pulled and can't even stop it, instead of you controlling it, it's holding you down. How can you stop something when you don't know what it is or understand it? Several months of being invaded, feeling violated, this thing wasn't playing at all. Every morning when my eyes open is moment everything starts. The moment I wake up, tiredness is there. During this time, hardly any movements, and finally, there were no movements, and I didn't even have the strength to try to move. Tiredness turned into extreme exhaustion. Think about it; no one likes to lose strength, especially when you wake up. This unknown thing has a purpose to take over me. I'm trying to come from within this. The more I try, the more it fights against me. My whole body went under this control, and I couldn't even wiggle my fingers nor move at all.

"Can you imagine wanting to get up but can't, wanting to talk, but can't?" Living in a place of unknown, how did these come into existence? My words are silent. My speech is silent. Can't cry, can't yell out, no physical pain, just a place within the unknown, desperately searching for a way out of this unwanted place. The reality of this was there's no way out from under until it let me up. I had no choice but to welcome the unwanted stranger. That annoying stranger that overstayed everytime. "Lord Jesus, help me!" I keep wondering, why did it choose me? How do you tell someone about my situation? When you know they want more details. Why does it keep capturing me? I'm just a prisoner to my own body. Think about it, there are no movements, you are in the middle of this unwanted stranger. There I am, laying in bed, can't speak, emerge in it, trapped in it, surrounding me, and refuse to let me go. I can do only four things: breathe, see, think and hear. There's no voice to speak, there's no movement to move, but you are right there, trying to come from under the hold.

I heard this small still voice saying, "Debbie, do something. This thing is not going to leave you alone. Open your mouth, and talk to your Momma before it's too late. You see, each day now lasts longer. You're going to have to speak out. Move Debbie, before someone finds you in here, can't move or talk. You know, they're going to panic if they find just laying in here." The small voice was speaking loud and clear, so loud I answered back and said, "Okay, tomorrow morning I will." Now, I didn't want to bother anyone. After all, people were going to ask questions after questions, already tired and frustrated. The voice says, "Give the details of what happened, this will cause your Momma to think, and she will know this isn't right. Debbie, you don't have to endure this alone. Your Momma will know this shouldn't be happening, but you have to open up your mouth and talk." I began to ponder over this, trying to put all the pieces together, making my words count. Unsure whether or not this will be my last try to say or do anything now. The uncertainty is wearing me out, carefully choosing the right words, so my talk would be short, now in bed, hoping, hoping for a new day of no unwanted stranger. I'm trying to believe that this will be gone, so there will be no reason to talk with my Momma. The new day is here, and of course, it was waiting for me to open my eyes. I heard my Momma calling me, "Debbie, Debbie sees what this boy wants; Debbie, get up now." "Sorry Momma, but I can't come now," addressing her in my mind. "You have to wait until this thing releases me, then I will come to you. "Hello Momma." Now Debbie, I know you heard me calling your name. Where were you? Why did you not come to see what I wanted?"

"Well, after you took so long, I went on and took care of him." Momma was very talkative and I needed Momma to be quiet and listen. Saying, "Okay, Momma, I need to talk with you. Listen to me." Momma looks at me, and begins to notice something wasn't right. I looked straight into her eyes and said, "Momma, I'm sick. I've heard you calling my name, but I couldn't come to you." Momma began to lean on the kitchen counter and said, "What do you mean, Debbie? "Momma, when I wake up in the morning, I am just here. Laying down, can't move, can't talk, and feeling exhausted; the more I've tried to move, the more tiredness and exhaustion come on, and finally, no movement at all. I hear you, but I just couldn't come." At this time, I am trying my best to remain calm, trying not to cry. "Momma, something needs to be done; it is taking longer now. I need a doctor." We both were trying to hold the tears back, and I could see the look in her eyes. Momma was worried, her countenance had changed, and she was stunned. "Debbie, go rest now, and when Hosea comes home from lunch, we'll see what we can do." "Okay, Momma."

Desperately Waiting

Hoping everything will be alright, but in my mind, I couldn't help thinking about what my Daddy is going to say. Knowing him, "Why did it take Debbie so long to say anything? She knew she didn't have to wait? Why that poor child felt that she had to wait?" At this time, I wasn't working. But, in this situation, help is needed. I had a problem; Daddy, can you please hurry up from work? Your baby girl is getting more scared and tired now. More anxious now than ever. How will I handle this load? I am not okay, getting more desperate every moment. Where do I go from here? Trying not to panic, so nervous, now I'm folding my arms and rocking back and forth, sitting on the side of my bed, trying to hold myself down. Daddy come on! I don't know what to do, I need to rest, but I'm too scared to sleep now. I need to be up, and this thing makes you tired even when you're up now. Oh, I can't take this; I need to go, feeling an urge to leave. Trying to calm down, taking deep breaths, speaking to myself, saying, "Help is on the way, relax, you can do this, Debbie. Slow down, lay down, you're going to be okay."

The moment finally arrives; my Daddy is home now. Wondering how Momma will tell him, will she let him eat first or tell him later? Either way, I am glad now. I don't mean to bother my family, desperately in need of help, so tired of trying to figure this out on my own. All of a sudden, the walls were thin, and I could hear clearly. The tone in Momma's voice just brought tears to my eyes. She said, "Hosea, Debbie is sick; she did not come to me when I called her." My Daddy said, "Eva Mae, what do you mean that child will not come to you? Have you seen her and talked with her? Hosea, Debbie said she couldn't get up; she can't move.

I could hear him saying, "Eva Mae, that poor child is sick, you know that's not like Debbie. You make that child a doctor's appointment." Momma asks him, "Hosea, when can you take her?" Daddy said, "Eva Mae, you make that appointment, don't worry about anything else, and that child needs to see the doctor right away." I could feel their love from a distance but was still afraid of the unknown. Desperately trying not to give in to the panic, waiting made me more nervous and wondering what I might have, how they can fix it, and how long it will take.

At this time, an uneasy feeling trying to calm down and not knowing what the doctor will find. In my mind, I kept thinking something is wrong; my heart was saying you are not all right. Momma schedules the doctor's appointment. In my mind, the doctor's appointment was too far off, and it seemed impossible for me to wait. I'm tired, restless, and still trying to be strong, but this holds me back. Momma, will you please make another appointment? One thing, Momma is a praying woman, unfortunately, just feeling so awful.

New approach today, planning on convincing Momma to call and change the appointment for an earlier date. Lord, help Momma to understand. I don't know how to shake this thing off—believing for a breakthrough to come soon. Understand, still in church and the man of God preaching and teaching the Word. There's a crisis in my life; Debbie needs help wondering what I will tell the doctor about my condition? I don't want him to think I am losing my mind, just in need of relief. I am feeling frustrated, tired, disgusted, and just need peace of mind. Reaching out to Momma, "I don't mean to worry or bother you. Look at me, this is hard, I know you is praying, but I don't know how much I can endure this. Momma, it's wearing me down now; I need you to call. If necessary, let me talk, and I need help. I'm doing all I can do to hold on; it's just hard for me now. So tired of waking up tired." Momma is listening to me now.

"Momma, I don't mean to disrespect you, but I am going through this, not you, Momma. You need to talk with the nurse, not the receptionist, convince her, and the nurse will talk with the doctor. That's how I will see the doctor right away." Momma is now speaking my language; she's talking with the receptionist, informing her that her daughter needs to see a doctor soon. I know they can move the appointment to another day, earlier than your schedule, even if you have to schedule with another doctor because this is worrying me. I know she needs to see someone within a couple of days. I can tell she's not well at all now, she is too tired, and I can't help her. The receptionist was trying not to make another appointment. I'm listening to the conversation. I spoke up and said, "Momma asked to speak with the nurse. That lady can't help you." I could tell the receptionist didn't like how Momma talked to her, but Momma wasn't backing down. I could hear the desperation in Momma's voice, and it was so touching that it brought tears to my eyes. Little did we know a nurse was listening to the conversation; she asked the receptionist to get permission to talk with Momma. The nurse apologizes for listening in on the phone call.

The nurse said, "I believe this doctor here can help her. Can I speak to her?" Momma said, "Debbie, this nurse wants to talk to you. She wants to know if it's alright." I informed her, "Yes, I can talk." Nurse, "Ms. Morrow? "Yes." I understand you're not feeling well." "Yes." When you wake up in the morning, you are exhausted. I want to talk with a doctor here. I believe he can help you. Do I have your permission to speak with him about your situation, and if he says he will see you, I will make an appointment for you and call you back. I am sure he will see you, and if he can't help you, he will find someone who will. He's a good doctor who cares about his patients. Do you agree to see him?" "Yes." The nurse called back and said, "The doctor will see you. Ms. Morrow, I got to tell you the doctor was amazed. I usually don't speak for anyone, but the doctor agrees to see you because of your illness. Take care, we will see you on your appointment day." Good news for me; so glad to hear, even if this doctor cannot help, he will find someone who can. Now I feel better knowing someone understands. When we receive more information, then I'll inform everyone? Meanwhile, there's hope for me, and I can take comfort in this now.

The Doctor Appointment

T he day of the doctor's appointment has arrived. Trying to keep calm but feeling anxious again; at least there is a name now. The doctor finally came into the room, "Ms. Morrow, my nurse informed me you haven't been feeling well for several days, and she thinks I can help you. What do you think about that?" "I hope that you can, sir." "Ms. Morrow, can you share with me what's been happening to you?" "Sure. It all started when I opened my eyes from sleep; I would be so exhausted at this point, I cannot move. If I try to move, more exhaustion occurs, but there is no movement. I cannot get up, and I cannot pull myself up." Doctor, "So what you telling me, no matter what you try to do, nothing happens?" "Doctor, nothing happens." Doctor, "How does that make you feel? Do you get frustrated, scared, tell me actually what is going on at that moment?" "Tired, frustrated, scared, don't know what to do." "Doctor," "Well, it's morning now, tell me, how are you feeling at this moment?" "I'm tired."

"Are you frustrated? Are you in pain anywhere?" "My hands and knees. Doctor, "Are they hurting now?" "No, Doctor." "When do they hurt you? When moving around? Like getting up and down? Trying to lift something?" "I do not have to do anything." Doctor,

"Is it bothering you?" "Yes, it just bothers me." Doctor, "Well, while you are here, I will run some tests on you; if that's okay? "That's okay." "Try to relax, the nurse will be here shortly, and she will take good care of you. I think I know what's going on, but let me finish with everything, and then we will talk about the result of the tests and examples." The nurse returned to the room. "Ms. Morrow, the doctor ordered a urinalysis laboratory using different types of blood work, an MRI, and a test to look at the head from the toes. He will be back in to do a physical exam and provide you with more information regarding his findings. Are you alright?" "All right."

The doctor enters the room again, "Ms. Morrow. I will examine your joints in your arms, knees and see if your body has maintained fluid. Now let's get started, okay. How are you doing now?" "Feeling a little tired Okay, I won't be long," "Ms. Morrow looks like you have some swelling in your knee; do you ever have any trouble bending them?" "No, just brother me at times, okay." "Well, all of my tests are in; as you see, the nurse just brought them in. According to all of my tests, I believe you have SLE. I want you to understand; you did not do anything wrong. It's just one of those things that occur. The study showed it does affect African Americans, Native Americans, and Asians the most. SLE causes you to feel the way you do."

"We will not discuss it now. After the blood work comes back, we will discuss everything then. To properly diagnose, we are going to send your blood to California to the Lupus Foundation. This place specializes in lupus. They will analyze your blood for me and tell me whether you have lupus; meanwhile, I will prescribe medicine for the swelling. It should be back within two weeks. If you have any other problem other than what you have now, call me. I will see you or write you a prescription and you can pick it up. Okay, thank you, thank you, Ms. Morrow." Going on two weeks now, worrying about the finding and something within me kept telling me something is wrong. They have not returned my call, and I haven't heard from them; in my mind, it was taking too long. My family was saying, "Nothing is wrong, no news is good news."

I knew there was something wrong within my heart, and I couldn't shake the feeling. Today I decided to call and talk with the nurse to see if they heard anything. One thing is for sure; I don't particularly appreciate waiting. I wouldn't say I like waiting at all.

Meanwhile, talking to the nurse, the doctor overheard our conversation. I could hear everything they were speaking about regarding me. The nurse thought she placed me on hold. "Doctor, this was your responsibility. Now, you find her a doctor, and that poor woman has been waiting all of this time." The nurse responded, "Doctor, I've been looking around. It is hard to find a doctor who will see her right away. They are busy and trying to find one who is willing to take your test." The doctor responded, "No, they could take her test, they don't have to put her through anything unnecessary, and this lady has been through enough. In this case, locate a doctor who specializes in Lupus patients. Call the Rheumatologist doctor, and he will know how to manage her treatment and understand her. Apologize to her and explain to her."

"Ms. Morrow, I am sorry for taking so long. I've been working on finding you a doctor, but everyone I've spoken with could not see you right away. The appointment was just too far off. I've informed the doctor, and he has advised me to find another doctor who handles Lupus patients and will be getting back to you shortly. Again, I am sorry this took a long time." My response was that, "It's okay, so I have lupus?" "Yes, the doctor who you will be seeing specializes in this. The doctor wanted him to inform you because he can give you more information on it. He didn't want to put you through any more unnecessary stress. He felt it would be better to see the other doctor instead of bringing you back here. Did the test result show lupus?" "Yes, instead of coming here, the doctor believes the other doctor can help you, and he doesn't want to put you through any more than he has to. Okay? Thank you, thank you, Ms. Morrow." After all, I have been through, you know, it seems like they would have called to inform me they are still searching for a doctor.

You've thought waiting is now easy, no it's still the unknown factor in my life. "Momma, what did they say?" "They have been trying to find a doctor who will take the doctor's result, and they are now going to use a rheumatologist who deals with lupus." "So when is the appointment?" "The nurse will call back and confirm with me in a couple of days, and she is still working on finding one. Okay? Debbie, we will still believe that she will find one, and you try not to let it get you down. You need to be calm, but we all can pray and pray that everything will be okay." On day two, the nurse called and said, " I've found you a doctor. The doctor wants to know where you want to come, to his office in Tyler, Texas, or Longview, Texas." My response was Longview, Texas, because it was close. "Your appointment is scheduled now in Longview, Texas. The doctor has sent your file over to review, and the new doctor will take it from there. We hope you get to feel better soon, Ms. Morrow, and thank you for your patience."

Doubting Debbie

N ow, you probably say Debbie is believing God's because she's in a church. Well, that might be so, but at this moment, for me to believe God is going to heal me from a disease completely, I don't know. After all, everyone I knew that says God is a healer was going through with their illness. So for me to say God is going to heal me from lupus wasn't easy to believe. My parents kept me in church, but the understanding about God as a healer wasn't there. If the pastors, ministers, deacons could sing, they could have my full attention in church. Preaching and teaching I didn't care for, and I didn't like. Sunday school, singing. Youth department singing. They all taught the lessons, but I only remember the songs.

There was no foundation for me to stand on. I was the one, who says, Preacher; you need to sit down. You are preaching too long; of course, I only said this to myself. That's why transformation had to occur. My mind had to change that with God; all things are possible. That's what makes my relationship unique to God, getting to know who he is for me. You see, in the younger days of going to church, pastors weren't teaching or preaching on relationship with God the Father. In my heart, I knew I had to have more than what the church was offering me about their God. During these younger days, I didn't care for the Word of God when God is the Word. No one taught me about God's wanted relationship with His people until my young adult life. Before lupus came into my life, I've given Jesus my heart; this is why I can say I fell in love with Him. I've made my confession. That if thou shalt confess with your mouth the Lord Jesus, and shalt believe in your heart that God hath raised him from the dead, they shall be saved. For with the heart one believes unto righteousness, and with the mouth, confession is made unto salvation [Romans 10:9-10 New King James Version]. Growing more spiritual but still had doubts about God being the healer. I told you, I've loved my church, but I had so much in me that needed fixing, and God was the only one who could clean me up. Not the doctors, Momma, my family, nor the church family; it was God and in His timing. I didn't know how God was working all of this out for my good.

Through this unwanted stranger, my life had to change. God is the head of my life. My walk changes and my talk changes, but my heart once doubted a savior who can completely heal. Now I know some healing is instantly, and some healing is a process. No matter what, Jesus does heals us. Sometimes, we might not see our healing, but keep the faith until we see the full manifestation of your healing. God's written words declare in Isaiah 53:5 King James Version: "But he was wounded for our transgressions, he was bruised for our iniquities: the chastisement of our peace was upon him; and with his stripes we are healed. All of those agony, pain, sickness upon himself. Praise the Lord, Jesus endured for you and me. One promise that would never change for us, Jesus forgives us of our sins, all that we had to do was make him Lord in our life, and learn of him." I've known God before the invasion came, but yet, why Lord? Why this pathway? Why me? I am not going to preach this to you, but these things I had to learn from them, and it brought me into a relationship with God.

Something In the Fire

L iving in the country, most families had Woodburner stove heaters where you add wood and make your fire to keep your home warm during the winter months. However, making the fire for the heater could be scary. Sometimes the fire would start, and sometimes nothing happens; this is why I don't particularly like making the fire.

Demonstration of making the fire for the heater: All wood stacked behind the heater; bring your kindling. The kindling is the small pieces of pine wood to use to help start your fire. Since we had a cast-iron wood-burning stove, it was a little different. Open the front part of the heater, add kindling, add wood and close the front door. Next, open up the top of the heater and pour kerosene on top of the wood, make sure some would run down to the kindling, and make sure the wood is not stacked tight because you need air to circulate. Next, scratch the match and when you see it, ignite and have a good firer close the door, and it will burn to keep the house warm. Unfortunately, the fire went out. I had to open the front door and stir the fire with an iron hook, and this let me lift the wood and jab in the fire. The fire was out. I didn't want to restart the fire, but I had no choice. After lifting and jabbing in the fire, I closed the front door and opened up the top; next, I poured in some more kerosene and scratched the match. Get this! The enemy was in the fire; what do I mean? I did not close the top of the heater, nor couldn't believe what I was seeing. It was beautiful, and it captured my attention. I have been pulled into its beauty. Colors were bright yellow, orange, and blue small flames, but it wasn't on top of the wood nor by the kindling. The fire was in the back of the heater but yet in the corner. Fascinated at the fire, no smoke, turning my head as to saying inward this doesn't seem right, and how did it come in back of the heater? While I'm looking at the fire, the fire was burning on the wood. Suddenly, the fire blazed up from the heater, and I felt a push; my head went backward. Here's the other notable thing, I didn't throw my head back, but that act awakened me from the fire's attraction. I looked down, and there was the kerosene jug by the heater. Do you realize there could have been a fire? I heard this voice saying, "I kept you from getting burned in your face; I was the one who made your head move. I saved you from the enemy. He planned to burn you by burning your face up. That's a reason to give praise."

Remember, there are lessons to learn during your spiritual journey. God was dealing with me in praise and thanksgiving. In everything give thanks: for it is the will of God in Christ Jesus concerning you (1 Thessalonians 5:18 King James Bible). "Father God, I thank you for helping me, for not letting the fire reach my face to burn it. Thank You, Jesus, hallelujah." And both hands went up in gratitude. When I thought about what just happened, I was happy and looked up with hands in the air, saying, "Thank you, thank you."

The Unfolding of the Unknown

Now the fear of the unknown is finally unfolding. How will I deal with the truth? How far does this have to play out now my reality has arrived? I don't feel those prayers at all. The moment I stepped through those doors, I knew my life would never be the same anymore. My downhill and downfalls were just around the corner, waiting on me. Momma and the neighbor were there, but there was nothing they could say to encourage me. Today brought back panic and feeling overwhelmed. Jesus, don't you leave me now. The nurse called my name, and it seemed like I couldn't move, but the reality was I don't want to walk through those doors. The nurse called my name again, thinking I want to go home now, lending forward but not getting out of the chair, trying not to be scared, and trying not to cry. Oh, it's just not right I can feel it. Fearful of what the doctor is going to say. Within my mind, saying "Momma, can we please go home? Let's get out of here."

The fear is more present than ever before. All of a sudden, "Debbie Morrow, are you here?" Closing my eyes, taking a deep breath, "Yes, I'm here." The nurse said, "It's okay, relax. Today, he's just going to inform you and talk with you." That was a relief, so I thought. In walked the doctor introducing himself and tells me the nurse will come back in to do an exam, and shortly, he will be back in. Relax Ms. Morrow." I don't know how they thought I was going to relax, with the unknown facing me.

"Hello Ms. Morrow, I am the doctor's nurse, every time you visit him, you will see me. The doctor wants to do an exam, just the regular exam like blood pressure reading stuff like that, if it's okay with you, okay? Ms. Morrow before, I came into the room, I've read your file your doctor sent over. I see he sent your blood to the Lupus Foundation, which is fine. I also went over the nurse assessments." After the evaluation was over the doctor walked in. "I only have a few of my own to perform, if that alright with you?" "Yes."

"How is the inflammation medicine working, and do you have pain in your joints?" "Yes." "I notice some swelling in your hands and knees. "Do they bother you at all?" "I do have some pain, and yes, they do swell up, but I still can move." "About your mornings, is it hard to get up?" "Yes, I can't move until it lets me move." "All right, I will prescribe you another medicine to use with what you're taking, which will help with pain and swelling. Take it as the bottles stated; if for any reason you need more, I will bring you back in so we can manage your care."

"Ms. Morrow, can I call you by your first name?" "Sure." "Debbie, this is your first visit here, and because it is your first visit, you must understand what is going on with you, okay? After carefully reviewing your file and what took place today and by the blood sample sent to the lupus lab, you do have lupus. The reason I started this way is because Lupus patients deal with it a lot. As we go through, I will ask if you understand. If you don't understand something, it usually takes up to two visits before the patient understands this. Rest assured, this isn't anything that you cause. There are so many out of a certain number of African American, Native American, and Asian cultures. At your age, the range usually is higher than yours. But we are here now. There are two types of lupus, and you have what is called SLE, which is already in the next stage."

At this time, I am looking at him, saying, "woah doctor, woah. I know I am sick, but not that sick. You have the wrong patient here, doc. I am not that sick." I don't know what he is saying because that's just not my file. Doc, hold on, hold on. Let me see that file, Doc? You have the wrong patient here. I need to look at the file name, no way." The doctor is sitting by my side, which means I can lend over to read this file name. I lean over, DEB; that's okay, that could only be Deb.

Leaning again, DEBB, that's okay that can be Debby; nope, that's not Debbie. You'd better look again; Debbie, well. I have to see the last name, leaning again; MO, that could be Moe. Lending again, this time sitting up and leaning over, because I need to get a good look. I just got to find out; MORR, safe, no wait for a minute girl, that's getting close to your name now, this could be Morris. Just one more look; here goes Debbie Morrow. Bingo, that's you, that you. Lord, I didn't know I was that sick.

I am about to pass out now. I hear the doctor calling my name, "Ms. Morrow, Ms. Morrow, are you alright." I looked at him and wanted to say, Doctor after all of what you said, no, I'm not alright now. The doctor reached out his hand and patted my hand. I remember thinking, Doctor, you're going to have to do more than pat these hands. The doctor was saying something I found unacceptable. How did it come to this in a short time because I'm getting ready to pass out or something? The next thing, I hear the doctor, "Debbie, Debbie, I am here!Take your time! Breath, you can do it, you can do it, I am here for you." It came to me, "Girl you better get a grip on yourself. Do you realize you are in the doctor's office? You don't want him to send you any other place than your home. You need to come to yourself. You can do this, Debbie, take a deep breath." The doctor, "Let's start over. I don't know how much you've heard, and I need to make sure you've understood everything."

"Debbie, you have Lupus Erythematosus, short name SLE. This kind attacks your immune system. We don't know why it attacks as it attacks; it attacks your good cells and bad cells. Debbie, I need you to know that there is no cure for this, and most Lupus patients suffer. I will share what you will be going through, but it doesn't look good for you. Some patients live a long time, and some don't. We can't explain it, and it's just how it happens for some patients. I cannot say you will live a year, six months, or three months because lupus has a way to creep up on an individual. If you get past all of this, you will make it, but there is no cure, so you will have to endure this for the rest of your life." Oooh! I need this man to quiet now. "You're okay, Debbie? "Yes." I am just telling this doctor a story. No, I am not okay. I know this doctor can see this. There's no way I am fine. How could I? Debbie! Yes, I know my countenance has dropped. "Now, let's go over some of the symptoms, okay. You can lose your hair," thinking that it's okay I can wear a wig. "Your hands can turn blue, pale, or purple, and when they turn, they will not turn back."

"We called this type Raynaud's Phenomenon." "That's okay, I can wear gloves." "There will be times that your fingers will be jumping, meaning moving because of the muscle causing them to move." "That's okay; I will grab them and hold them when I can." "Your joints will become stiff." That's okay. I will use DW40 motor oil; my grandmother uses it all the time now. "The weather will be a problem for you now." "Oh!" "Yes, try to stay out of the sun; sunlight makes the rashes hurt. There are two different kinds of rashes; a butterfly rash has its shape like a butterfly across your nose and cheeks. I'm afraid you will receive the other one called wolf bite, and those who receive this type stay at home. Those who have this kind of bite, realize they can't wear anything over their scars. They found out it's better to leave uncovered, because it makes it hurt too badly when covered." Wait a moment, when the doctor said lupus was related to a wolf, I thought the doctor was losing his mind— thinking to myself, "How this wolf bite will appear on my cheeks. What is this doctor talking about, tiny bits? Little more, I'm going to be coming up out of his office. I didn't sign up for this." All of a sudden, "Ms. Morrow let me explain this. That's how the face will look; it just resembles the wolf bite. The Latin word for lupus means wolf." Now in my mind, who wanted to be related to any form of wolf. It's not over yet; I'm sitting in this chair, in the doctor's office, trying to imagine wolf bites on the cheeks. All I could see was my face disfigured with all of those tiny bites that looked like they would never heal. At this moment, I didn't care whether these small bites looked dry or running. It was just going to be a horrible thing to look at from day- to- day. The doctor had already said this kind doesn't leave, and covering it up only worsens, so it was just going to be unacceptable. Think about it already hurting, and now wolf bites and people will stare. I don't need this, that's just more hurt on top of hurt, I don't like this outcome.

"Now, this does affect your brain? Your mind?" "There will be days where you will not be able to remember anything at all. I see you have a son. "Yes." "Because of how this lupus works, do you have a living will?" "No." "Okay, this is what I want you to do, while you're in your right state of mind, I need you to write a letter, before you close it you need to make sure you have everything you want in it because you cannot open it once it's sealed, okay." Now, put in your letter whom you want your child to stay with, whom you believe can raise your son since there is no will, the judge will honor this request. Make sure you don't open it. Next put the letter into a place where you know someone will find the letter or tell someone you trust. They cannot open the letter, okay."

"Start keeping a journal and write down everything. Writing in the journal will help me and the psychiatrist pinpoint where your mind starts to leave you. So you will need a psychiatrist. Remember, nothing you have done; this attacks your immune systems; it's like they are fighting against each other."

"Next, I need you to promise me something, okay? Once you begin to lose your mind, or forget how you made it somewhere and don't know how to leave, promise me from that point on you will not go out by yourself, Debbie. You can easily get turn-around and can't come back. When this happens, someone will have to find you. I am sharing with you this happens because the mind gets confused.

Promise me, you won't let this happen to you?" "I promise." "Okay, I know that it seems to be a lot, but there is still more." "Okay." "Don't worry about what has been said, because we will go over this again for the next two visits. I found out this way. It helps patients to understand it better; let's move on. "Okay."

"Your muscles will be moving on their own; this will cause you to be jumping. When you realize before this occurs, you're having trouble with standing, walking. That's the time to move everything close to you because it will be a problem. Only rest when you need to, because this disease we call creeps up on you when laying down, it will keep you down, just get up, when you feel it." "Okay."

"There will come a time when you will have to dope yourself up due to the ringing of your ears. This sound will be very loud and annoying. Debbie, you will want relief from the sounds. Unfortunately, this is when you need to use the medicine to dope yourself up. I am going to teach you how to do this." "Okay." "Say if you are already on this med, and you'll hear the noise, take another pill. After you take that pill and the noise is still there, take another pill. Now say you've taken six pills, but that noise is not letting up, you take another pill. You need to understand that this dose can go up to eight or more pills. I want you to understand when it gets to a certain level, you will not recognize anyone and probably be speaking out of your head because of the high dose."

"Now here's how you come down from those doses. You can't do what you did before. Say you have taken eleven of those pills today, then you decrease that dose, only by one pill. The next day you reduce it again. You gradually wean yourself down. Now say that you are down to six pills, but the noise comes back, increases just like before, and now when it's time to come off from where you're at. Gradually decrease as before. When you have increased enough, you will not feel anything or know anyone, keep this in mind." "Okay."

"All of your body organs will shut down, which is how we know you will not pull through." Now, I know I didn't hear the doctor right; about my body. My body is not going to shut down. I don't think so.

I am not accepting this fact. No, doctor, something is wrong with this picture. "Debbie, the doctor is still talking with me!" "When they get to this stage, their caregiver can't take care of them anymore. The patient will go to a facility in Shreveport to stay until they pass or make a recovery. I want you to know we are here for your family as well. Now some caregivers take care of their own, and some cannot tolerate it."

"You will have to wear a pamper because you will not be able to move. They will change you and feed you, make sure you will have some food and water by your bedside, this way, if you can feed yourself, I need for you to eat. Even just a little provides you with energy, eating even when you don't have an appetite. Now, when you are flat on your back and can't talk or move, your eyes will be moving on their own. Now your eyes can be fixed in one way like you're staring at something. That is just what happens to some patients and you will not be able to control your eyes. Once your eyes are fixed, they are fixed."

"We are here for you and your family." Leaving the room, now in despair, trying to hold my head up, trying to put a smile on my face, I walk right by Momma and our neighbor in the waiting area. I went to the restroom and, on the way back, made my appointment. What am I going to do now? Tell me, how did I get here? How do you tell your family what the doctor said? I just felt like I received a death sentence! How do you say goodbye? Feeling like the bottom just fell from me, now feeling low, broken. I know everyone is waiting for me to share, but I don't want to. Feeling hurt from within, can't run from it, more hurt now. I find myself with nowhere to run. Opening up both hands and placing my face in my hands, and shaking my head all at the same time. "Lord Jesus, help me, help me."

Momma, "Debbie, if you talk about it, you will feel better." I just kept quiet, wiping every tear from my eyes. I wanted to boo-hoo out loud so bad, but kept it all in with frowns on my face. How do I get my immune systems to stop fighting against each other? Why can't my body work, right? Why? What went wrong? How can this be the red cell fighting against the white cell, the white cells fighting the red cell? I don't understand. Could all of those seizures affect the body, or could it be how my parents keep me from biting my tongue during these seizures? "Debbie, why are you putting yourself through this? They told you nothing you did to cause this, girl. You need to accept it and move on."

You tell me, how can I accept what I can't receive? So, desperate trying to figure this out. So confused, just hopeless now. Everywhere I turn, there it is, just feeling more trapped within, everywhere I look, there is no way out of this. I was more frustrated than ever, trying to push through, but I can't get my head right from what the doctor said about this disease. The only thing I could tell Momma is that there's no cure for this lupus. I can't talk about it. I just laid down, to rest curled up in bed, wrestling with myself, saying over and over, there is no cure, no cure, no cure.

O' me, tears are just rolling down my face. Feeling defeated now, yep, faith is gone, don't see my way out. Just hurt beyond the agony. I don't know what to do now. My anger has wholly turned. I can feel the anger raging up inside of me. Trying to calm down, but I can't calm down. Hurting, whoever thought a person who hurt so bad I don't see tomorrow? I don't see myself with my son. So in bondage now, I feel like my hands are all tied up, nowhere to turn. Who wants to live and doesn't know they are in the world? I will not be able to recognize my child and will not know his name. I can't feed or clothe myself, need help with the bathroom, have to wear pampers, muscles jumping all over the place, drooling, eyes going back and forth and when they stop that their fixed one way. Wolf bites in my face, sunlight and cold weather harm me. A time when I have to dope up, and then dope down, can't talk, can't move. Who wants this type of lifestyle? Living from one day to another day of not knowing anything, God help me! I can't lose this picture now it is within. There's no way I am going to endure uncertainty. No! I have done nothing unto nobody, nobody Lord. I've tried to live the Word, tried the best I can. I'm not the same person I once was. But here am I, alone and frustrated, tired, and scared, supposed to take it.

The Hidden Secret

Today I thought about living my life without being in the right frame of mind. Could I do this terrible thing that was placed upon me, not knowing anyone, just living in all types of pain? Not fitting in, living within this unknown world of despair, alone and rejected by God and my family, church family, and friends. Do I want anyone to see me like what I am supposed to become? One thing for sure, I do know, I don't want to live like this and don't want my family to make any decision for me when it comes. With everything happening, if things weren't going to get any better, then I need a plan, whether to end my life or not. How was I going to do this? I do not want to deal with any pain in the process. Need it to be quick. Don't want to be by myself. Who could I get, and who will do it for me? Where is the place? What time will it happen? Come on, Debbie, think who that person is! After finding the way to end my life, the only solution was to find a double-barrel shotgun. Next, find a person who can live with what they do, especially after pulling the trigger. Already knowing where two double-barrel shotguns are, I need the perfect location; I have the ideal place by the house, in the pasture under the big shade tree, unfortunately, anyone from home could look out from the kitchen window. I rather lose my life than linger on here and not be myself or not knowing anyone, including me. I picture myself dropping my head down and falling to my knees, but facing the shooter and falling over on the ground.

Now you are thinking, church girl, who's getting the word and planning on ending her life. Yes, I didn't have the nerve to do it and be by myself. This way, it was only going to take one shot. I never plan on being shot in the head. The perfect place was the heart, you know, the chest. I need my family to recognize me to say they're proper goodbyes. I will not share this plan with the doctor. I don't want him to think I'm not myself. I will continue to go for doctor's visits but will not reveal this, for now.

Remember, I inform you how inappropriate I was to God at the beginning of this story, this is part two of my story and keep in mind God wanted it this way. Listen very carefully. What I mean, I had no strength to raise my head. Here's the thing, I could not look up or sideways. I had to turn my body around; and my eyes could look up, but my head remained down for several days now. I'm walking and talking, I can't move my head.

God has a way to get our attention. I'm still going to church, hoping no one noticed how I was walking. All of a sudden, "Debbie, you act as you can barely walk. Why are you walking with your head down? You need to look up, child! You need to see where you are walking and hold your head up! We are on the outside getting ready to go, Debbie; you better look up; you can't be walking with your head hanging down. You will knock things over, or someone or something will knock you down girl, stand up!" I believe it was the prayers of the righteous one that was helping me. No one knew what happened to me in the bathroom. Remember, I told God, here am I, take me now. My body wasn't my body. My body felt strange. It came to me, my body was trying to shut down, and He allowed me to feel how it feels. Yes, I believe God is in control. God is the one whos' all-powerful.

For some reason, there was no more tiredness for me; the body was feeling strange now, so weak, I could hear like never before, there was no floor under my foot for me to walk on. Let me explain. You know how light the eggshell feels once you crack it, that's how soft my footstep was. Everything within my body was saying that your body is closing down and nothing can stop it. Every day it is getting weaker and weaker now, barely getting up. God is doing this thing, and He's moving quickly. My body is so wearied, so fragile, could this be life getting ready to leave my body? After all, what I have done? Right now, I don't trust myself to stand or walk anywhere. I don't believe there is a tomorrow for me now. Maybe death is right around the corner now. I was lying in the wingback chair, with both legs over the arm. I could hear a small voice from a distance speaking to me, "Debbie, you need to do something now before it's too late. Ask God, tell God you want to live? You see you're having trouble. You are weak, don't you want to live?" "Yes, I want to live." At this point, I don't have enough strength to move my leg down, and if they got down too weak to get up and move, no walking here.

Suddenly, I heard the voice of God telling me to get up and go back to the place. Immediately the picture appeared of me standing in the bathroom, in the middle of the bathroom floor. It was hard to believe now; the words came from my mouth to hurt God. The shame and feeling of letting God down. How could I do God that way? Why didn't I calm down? Why the anger had to take over. The Holy Spirit brings convictions: Debbie, "you talk to God the Father like he's no one to respect. The same God you spoke to reaching out to you, but now your body is too weak to walk and stand. Debbie, let go of your pride. Can't you see, God is here waiting on you to undo what you have done. Don't pass up the opportunity. You know God is a forgiving God. It's you holding the grudge. Let it go. Why are you having all of these conversations with yourself, when you know God gives us his mercy and grace. Can't you sense his love? Don't you want to live? God never turned his back on you. You were acting from the place of hurt in your heart when you were diagnosed with lupus. After you realize what you have said, now you'll feel shame and hurt.

God still loves you and wants you to continue with him. Remember, you said you never knew God as a healer, everyone you knew still has their sickness. Here is the opportunity for you, but you need to act upon the opportunity by moving out and doing what God wants you to do. He's not going to leave you nor forsake you—it is not your way of handling things, but his way of doing things for us. Let it all go, the pride, hurt, humiliation, walk into forgiveness of yourself and God." "Next, saying too weak, can't make it there. I don't trust myself to stand." Instantly felt a strength within my body to move. Before I moved, I tested my strength to see, and I could move. Suddenly, I began to take deep breaths and move my hands and feet; it was God, I'm lending on now. Not my strength, but his strength. For the first time in a long time, my feeling toward God was returning to me. God provided the strength for me. So excited, I ran through our den down the hall into the bathroom. In the same direct place where I voice my rage, the anger out on God, I repented to God with a sincere heart. Telling God how sorrowful I was and asked if he could forgive me. I had no right to talk to him like he never matters to me, for I am sorry. I won't ever do it again. Telling him, I had no right to use my voice to speak against him—O' how I do need him and want him in my life. My life is not worth living without him. Asking him again forgive me for all of the emotions, hurt, and shame I display toward him. The moment I said I am godly sorrow and meant it from my heart. All of a sudden, my head came back up. I could turn it again. I thank the Lord for giving me another day. I don't know how this all will play out, but I am grateful to God. For his grace and mercy. After leaving the bathroom and sitting down, it suddenly came to me that something was still wrong. I got up and went looking out the window and looked up into the sky.

All of a sudden, I thought to myself, wait a minute! Something here doesn't feel right. Then it stood out; God did not remove this lupus from me. All I did was to repent. In other words, I had a change of heart toward my actions. Towards my way of thinking, and believe I was never going to behave as I did. Also, apologize to

God, telling him I am godly sorrow from the words and tune release from my mouth. What is God doing? In Psalm 32:8, Amplified Bible, "I will instruct you and teach you in the way you should go; I will counsel you [who are willing to learn] my eyes upon you." One thing for sure, not going back where I started in the bathroom speaking to God like he's no one. No!

I will not repeat that form of speech. Now I have a new problem; why didn't God heal me? Why do I have to wait for my healing? What was God's thinking? While looking out of the window, all of a sudden the bible appeared before me. God knows how to get our attention. God said, "When you go to bible class, have your pastor lay his hands on you and ask him to pray over you." The next three Wednesdays it snowed and bible class was canceled. Now, I am wondering if it will be too late to act upon God's instruction for Wednesday night.

God spoke and said, "I didn't tell you which bible class. I said, when you go, have him lay his hands on you and pray over you." Here I go again, thinking to myself, I am not going to ask him to do this! I had never experienced anything like this before, and God wanted me to ask my pastor to lay his hand on me. Now, there's just one problem I have. There will be people in the church, and I had to get up in front of everyone. God knows I'm shy and nervous standing in front of people. Why God? Couldn't you breathe on me or do something else and heal me? Why this way? Think Debbie, think, who do you know that will share what God has instructed you to do concerning bible class? This way, when bible class time, the pastor can ask me to come up in front and lay his hands on me and pray. Uh, let me think about who this person is. When it's bible class time, the pastor can call me out, and I would get up; that way, everyone will already know why and I don't have to ask the pastor.

Yep, the perfect plan. Now, I should have known better than to plot against God's plan. There I am, in bible class, waiting for the pastor, and the pastor did not call for me to come up. What have I missed? I'm at bible class and the pastor is getting ready to end bible class. Different people were getting my attention to go up there before he closed bible class. Finally, someone touched my shoulder and said, "Debbie, you need to go up and receive what God has for you. I know you feel good now, but you might not feel good later on and need to act upon what God has spoken to you now. Debbie, God wouldn't have spoken for the pastor to lay hands on you for no reason."

"Debbie follow through with God's plan before it's too late." Within me, there was an assurance of hope. Let me explain the assurance of hope; it brought joy and peace inside my being. The calmness I needed was immediately there. All of the missing pieces just fitted into the proper place. I believe God's love was there. There was no need to act upon what God said regarding the pastor to lay his hand on me and pray over me. Why? Because I felt good. This thing had begun to happen a week before bible class. It wasn't for me to alter the plan of how He has established for healing. When I turned around and looked, they were looking at me, nodding their heads to go upfront. My head went down, and I took a deep breath and eased my way up to the pastor. He asked if there was anything else from the floor or anyone. I went up to inform him what God had said, and then it finally took you long enough; that's the moment I knew he already knew whether they told him or God told him. We all laughed, and then he lay his hands and prayed over me.

My way was just going to the doctor and take medicines. God way was In (James 5:14 - 16 New Living Translation), "Are any of you sick? You should call for the elders of the church to come and pray over you, anointing you with oil in the name of the Lord. Such a prayer offered in faith will heal the sick, and the Lord will make you well. And if you have committed any sins, you will be forgiven. Confess your sins to each other and pray for each other so that you may be healed. The earnest prayer of a righteous person has great power and produces wonderful results."

God designed for some healing to take place; it was still God using a godly man to perform what needed to happen on earth as a point of contact with the believers to stir their faith and to bring things into his order.

Sharing With Loved One

I t probably seems unfair to me, but sometimes sharing is hard. I have been trying to find the right words to share without breaking down. Finally decided to share with the family, "Girl; you're not going to die. Girl, you heard wrong. Those doctors don't know everything. So, what you are just going to wait around here and die? What about your child, Eric? Do you believe this, Debbie? I sure hope not, and you know the doctors don't know everything. You know you should get a second opinion. Just ask them to refer you to another doctor, Debbie. There's nothing wrong with that, people do this all the time, and if you want him to treat you, that will be fine. Don't just do nothing." My response, "This was the second doctor, and both said the same thing." I will never forget when Momma informed my Daddy; I could hear her saying, "Hosea, Hosea." What is it, Eva Mae? "Debbie told us what all the doctors said." "Well, Eva Mae, what did he say?" "It is not good at all," it was a pause there, "Debbie can die from this." "Eva Mae, we will do all we can for her, now you hush-up, she'll be fine, and he went outside."

My heart broke because I believe he was trying to be strong for her. From that day on, I only shared with Momma what was happening to me—calling the pastor's home and talking with her, telling her everything the doctor said. Her response was, "Okay, I will inform him. Debbie, we will be praying for you and the church as well. We know the doctor's report is not God's report, right, right? We believe the report of the Lord; that's who reports we believe." My church family and friends were trying to figure this out as well. Lupus was something nobody knew. Everyone did their best to help me, but unfortunately, their help was limited. I didn't mean to be disrespectful because I had to deal with this unknown lupus, and it was scary and hard to embrace for a while. After the doctor told me everything about lupus, it was a while before I shared anything with my family, church family, and friends.

There I go back into my shell, this time, I need to be alone. I didn't think it would be so bad. I need time to face this, it seems like this will be the lifestyle for me. Who wants this type of lifestyle? Now I am holding my head down, just disgusted, torn up inside now. Mercy Lord, don't seem fair, but here I am, hurting bad, my life will never be the same again. Just not right at all. I don't understand; why can't I be the mom for my child? Why does our world have to change? And why can't I continue to live an entire life for you? I guess you know best, but for me, this is not the best life now. My sister is here, Debbie, get up. Why are you lying around the house? You know, if you get up and take a bath and fix yourself up, comb your hair, you would feel better. I knew she wasn't going to leave me alone. I went straight to the bedroom and looked at myself in the mirror, and convinced myself there's nothing wrong with me. I took my right hand and slicked my hair back, and went back to lay down. Nobody understood me.

Today the family is planning on doing something. I can hear them in the living room, "Momma, Debbie, why don't you go and see what they are doing? They are calling you." "Alright, here I come." When I made it in the living room, they were outdoors, and I was resting on the couch. Next, my sister said, "You act like you are waiting on something. Why are you still lying down? You look like you lost your friend, this is not you, you need to get up. Girl, you're not going to die. Stop waiting on death. Stop trying to die. Child, those doctors don't know everything, get up and move and pull yourself together. Get up from this couch and live, child, before it is too late." Those words, meet me where I was at. Stop waiting on death, live your life. It only took a minute before those words reached my soul. Especially stop trying to die.

How Do I Say Goodbye

"How can you say goodbye to the one whom you loved?" My heart breaks every time I think about saying, "Bye." What will be my first words? How will I say it? Will I open my mouth and speak, or will I break down and cry? Either way, it puts me in a complicated place. Whenever I imagine looking into their eyes, my heart melts, and then sadness comes. Saying bye isn't easy to do, especially when you love your family. I found myself wanting to hug my son and wrap my arms around him and tell him. I love my family, but trying to find the right words seems strange.

What is the right way to say bye? I don't want those words to be sorrowful. I believe saying those words to my parents, brother, and sisters will not be as difficult when I am ready. One thing is for sure, "I need to pull myself together. I don't want to be over-emotional." Today I decided to say all of my goodbyes. Hoping somehow it will make it easier to deal with the unfair illness called lupus. The thing is, whenever I get ready to say, "Goodbyes something always occurs. I don't know what to make of this, there is a stop. I believe someone, keeps me from releasing the words out of my mouth. How unfair?" I feel the need to tell everyone goodbye, but why am I trying to say it before the time? You know that does seem right; it's not time. Yet, every time there was a presence there, not let me say good-bye. "Oh well!" I guess when the right time appears, they all will be there.

Thinking to myself, "Debbie, pull yourself together, don't go before your time. Look around, there's still life, your blood is still running in your veins. You see, "God still has you here. Stay here, girl. Let God do it! "Reflecting on my speech to myself," Debbie move out of the way, stopped planning, stopped trying to figure everything out. Debbie, live your life; you have to come from within lupus. Don't let lupus keep you, don't let lupus control you. Turn it all around. You speak to it and tell it what you need it to do. Come on out before it's too late."

Enemy Launch His Attack

As I prepared to leave the bathroom, my right arm started to hurt. Trying to figure out where the hurt was coming from, "Why was my arm bothering me? I didn't recall hurting my arm before. Thinking to myself, "Girl, you need to do something." But what could I possibly do? Looking around, "Only me, standing in the middle of the bathroom floor." As I realized this agony pain is not going to stop, "How can this be? Again, I don't see anyone, so where is this pressure coming from? Who would do terrible things?" All of a sudden, it came to me that the enemy is causing this attack. Who is the enemy, the accurer of the brethren? The devil's plan is to steal, kill, and destroy us. The enemy keeps forgetting I am in God's hands, not his.

Trying desperately to stop this awful pain, not having any success. Nothing I can do to stop the pressure, no rubbing, no patting is helping, and no pleading is working. There's nothing else to do but, cry out to God, saying, "Help me, Lord. Help me, have mercy on me." The pain is not letting up. I find myself saying, "Stop, why don't you stop and leave me alone?" Meanwhile, this pressure is getting tighter and tighter. Suddenly, there was a shift, but the change wasn't leaving; its mission was to apply more pressure to my arm.

Instead of one, there were now two unseens enemies, one at the finger, and one was in the middle pushing down my shoulder and pulling down on my fingers. It felt like my shoulder was being pulled off. The pain was severe from both positions and now a pull above the elbow. The unseen enemy was working together to pull the arm off from my shoulder. I could sense someone was on the way because the unseen enemy had speeded up the process; it was like they knew someone or something was about to show up, so they had to hurry up trying to pull my right arm off. In my mind, I heard the 23rd Psalm, and immediately I began to say the 23rd Psalm.

"The Lord is my shepherd; I shall not want. For He maketh me to lie down in green pastures: he leadeth me beside the still waters. He restoreth my soul: he leadeth me in the paths of righteousness for his name's sake. Yea, though I walk through the valley of the shadow of death, I will fear no evil: for thou art with me; thy rod and thy staff they comfort me. I had to stop speaking this scripture; my mind went to where have you heard this scripture (wait a minute! This psalm preacher used for funeral purposes, and I am not going to die, not now. Then I immediately heard a small still voice saying, continue. Next; I began to pick up from where I left off from). Thou preparest a table before me in the presence of mine enemies: thou anointest my head with oil; my cup runneth over. Surely goodness and mercy shall follow me all the days of my life: and I will dwell in the house of the Lord forever [Psalm 23: 1 - 6 King James Bible]"

I believe the enemy knew God was going to rescue me. That's why the enemy tried to finish the attack in a hurry. After the attack, God showed me a vision and said, "Stretch forth your arm and speak what you hear from me." As I said what God said, people were crying, people around the stage lifted hands, people were surrendering to God." What are you talking about, Debbie? God was teaching me how to pray over thousands of souls at one time. I was amazed God chose me to do this.

In Deuteronomy 9:29 New International Version, "But they are Your people, Your inheritance, whom You brought out by Your great power and outstretched arm." God was preparing me for His ministry.

Lupus Exposures
and Triggers

Environment Exposures: Sun

The pain was agony. I never thought what God created would hurt me so badly. On this day, I went to the grocery store, and the sunlight was shining bright, and the rays of the sun made my neck and shoulder ache. The first thing I did was block the sunlight from my neck. Using both of my hands on my neck provided a shield of protection from the sun. The pain was severe, and it brought me almost to the ground. I threw my body against the door pulling upward so I could stand up.

The pain wasn't letting up. Suddenly, I heard a voice saying, "Go on inside; the sun causes this pain." Next, I began to push my way in, almost falling in. Now on the inside, bending over, I am looking to see if anyone is looking at me. When I turned to the left side and began to pull myself straight up, the grocery store lady said "madam, are you all right? Do you need any help?" About that time, another worker came up to her and asked her what she was doing. She informed her. She was looking at me because of the look on my face, and how I entered the store let her know something was wrong with me. The worker asked her, did she ask if she needed any help? She responded I told her I'm all right, but she knew something wasn't right, and that's why she was watching me make sure.

Environment Exposure: Cold Weather

I thought the sunlight was harmful, O' the cold weather was terrible and miserable. I just came from outside with a heavy coat trying to get in. The minute I went through the door, the cold air hit the back. I'm crying O', O.', O', O', trying to touch my back, hoping this will somehow release me from the pain. At this point, I couldn't reach my back, but trying to get to the woodstove heater, after all the pain was coming with the cold weather, I needed immediate release.

Exhaustion: Too Exhausted to Walk Through the Door

Whoever thought of leaving home feeling fine, and this occurs. There I was, standing on the porch, immediately it came, extremely exhausted. No strength to move, just standing still. I needed to go inside the house, but there was no voice to ask for help. There is no strength to raise the arms, not even the strength to knock on the door or turn the doorknob. I was standing in front of the door. All I could say from within, Lord, help me! Give me strength to go inside of the house. Help me, Lord Jesus. No one inside of the house knew I was on the outside waiting to get inside the house. It amazed me standing up and too exhausted to step through the door. Everyone was in the back room.

All of a sudden, my right arm went up, and I found myself catching the front doorknob, twisting and pushing it open. There I was still standing in the doorway, legs not moving, still no voice to yell out for their help, and no one came to the door. The next thing I realized, I was looking into the living room, still standing and trying to figure out how to get there and to which chair. Suddenly, I was carried into the house, led into the wingback chair because the other chairs were too low. Next, I turned around to sit down, and just when I began to sit down, I felt strength in both arms on the backside, on the back, and both legs. The next thing happened before I could sit down; there I was, standing straight up, no weakness, no exhaustion, just feeling good, actually too good. I found myself wanting to thank the individual for giving my strength back, so I began to look for the individual; no one was in the room with me. I am looking all between the chair cushion, beneath, around, on top of the chair. All I know, I need to say thanks. After realizing there was no one physically with me, it came to me. "Debbie, it was God who did those things for you." I threw up my hand and looked up and said, "Lord thank You. I thank you, thank you."

Muscle Trigger: Finger Movements

The index finger on the right hand is moving. After realizing this is going to be a part of my life now, it's just another thing I have to cope with dealing with Lupus. It wasn't easy to see the movements on one finger out of control. My index finger went from side to side, and I could feel the muscle moving the finger every time I held the finger with my other hand, trying to stop the finger from moving. Nothing works. If I squeeze the finger, it keeps right on moving. One day during the movement, someone was there. Here I go, trying to make sure the person didn't see the finger jumping. I realized what was taking place, but my heart was crushed, meaning I never wanted anyone to see my finger moving on its own. Hard to watch the frustration appear on my face because of the shame. There was no way for me to explain what was going on, but in my heart, I always believed that God knew my heart, and I didn't want to be humiliated. God honored my heart because the lady didn't know what was happening. Now, we served an amazing God!

Mind: The Episode of Memory Loss

D ealing with memory loss was one of the things that bothered me the most. However, this hardly happens, but when it does, it messes with me. The doctor had already informed, there would be times where I could easily misplace things. However, this will be one of the clues not to be by myself, always to have someone with me. I refuse to say I'm losing my mind. Whenever I share this story, how hard it is for me to remember where I put things, people, in general, will say, that's all right. Sometimes we forget where we put things and don't worry just when we don't expect it to show up. No one knew, I did lose a little memory. The little memory loss my family shared with me. They never knew, even when they were sharing, they had no idea.

Trying with everything within me saying that is not the same, I don't know why this is hard to understand when lupus patients share about not remembering. I figure it is better to be quiet. Something about this people can't receive. Wondering how to tell the doctor about this episode or do I wait? I think I will wait and pray it is not too late. After all, it's not all the time. I know the doctor wants me to keep a journal and bring it to the next office visit. The reason for this, he and the psychiatrist can see where my mind is now. I know this will help them, but I am not ready for anyone to say you'll lose your mind, and there is medicine for me to take when this occurs. Sometimes, I feel rushed.

Refuse To Dope Up:
Ringing in the Ears

The day finally arrives for me to dope myself up. The doctor has informed me what to do when I hear many noises. I said to myself, "This will not be my norm No, I refuse to dope myself up. God will help me through this." As tears ran down my cheeks, the noise became louder and louder. In my mind, thinking, "If I could get my mind off of this high pitch sound, I will be alright." I am now finding myself looking through my bedroom window, using both hands to hold my pillows over my ears. Frowns are in my face, eyes squinching due to the high volume of noise, wishing it would all stop.

Suddenly, I remember my momma saying, "When her blood pressure was up, it sounded like crickets." I wanted so badly to scream. Now I am wondering if these meds cause my blood pressure to go up? Also, wondering if this why the doctor wanted me to purchase a blood pressure machine? Whatever the situation might be, I now have to endure this problem for now.

Instead, I reminded myself to fight it, telling myself, you will be alright, hold on, don't stop. Keep on fighting, saying, "Lord help me get me through this." It's just hard to do, and the sounds were ringing out loud; nothing could drown that humming sound. It seemed like closing my ears just made it worse. Suddenly, the sounds were to the left and right of me, then surrounding me. My mind went back to a familiar song, where this lady was singing at church. I could hear part of the song. That song reached me from where I was in the most challenging time of my life. All I could hear was this verse over and over and over. That melody came back to me. I convinced myself, there is a reason why this song came to mind. You see, the more I sing this song: There's A Bright Side Somewhere by Rev. F. C. Barnes and Rev. Janice Brown. I realized this song was working on my heart. Here's the verse that minister to my soul:

> There's a bright side somewhere,
> There is a bright side somewhere,
> Don't you rest until you find it.
> There's a bright side somewhere.

The song inspired me to keep on searching, keep on looking for Jesus because Jesus is my bright side. Here is what made the song special; I didn't know the whole song. Sometimes all I could say was that there was a bright side somewhere. Just that one line over and over and over. I would talk to myself, telling myself hold on, Debbie, you hold on. Focus your attention on other things than the noise. Somehow those words came alive for me, and they provided hope and peace.

Yes, tears were running down my cheeks. Sometimes I had to get up from the bed and move around and look up and ask God to help get me through this ordeal. God became my strength. People ask me why that song, didn't you know it was Jesus before and now. They didn't understand; I needed for it to happen in this way for a reason. I was singing from my heart, and I needed these ringing ears to let go of me. Somedays, it would all leave, and some days it wouldn't, but I was able to hold on and not let the sound push me over to take the meds. There were days I cried myself to sleep, and the pillow wet from my tears. I didn't have to use meds. I thank God and praise him for all that He was doing. All that he has already done, and for who He is. Glory be to God! I learned to praise God; I am still here and in my right frame of mind.

Dreadful Nights: Hallucinations

O h, how I dreaded the nights. Those night times were frightening. I never thought of being fearful of going to bed. I was not fond of it at all. Every night, before bedtime, I went to the porch. Staring up in the sky, I looked, wondering if God would intervene. I didn't believe God was, so I dropped my head. I knew what nighttime means.

Another night in fear. One thing I didn't want to do; to open the door to my room and step inside because a nightmare was coming, and I couldn't stop it. I wanted to share with others so badly, but too scared they might think I'm losing my mind. It was fear every night, after night for two straight months. It was constantly occurring when I am just getting the rest. During the night, I would wake up and see snakes. I often wonder if it was just my mind or those pills. However, the case might be, I am awake.

My eyes were wide open. I couldn't believe what was in front of my face. There was no dream, and I would wake up and see giant long snakes coming for me on the ceiling and the bedroom walls. One on top of the door, one on the back wall, and two on the sidewall, and there I am in bed looking and watching them. My eyes are still open and more nervous. I was wondering what they were getting ready to do. Suddenly, they are moving, one by one, and they would dive down and swing toward me, and when they get close, they will go back. The next time, they would get into my face, diving down from the front and side, and would go back. Each one waited for their time, but they would always meet up together in the middle and return to their original post.

After a period of short time, all the snakes would leave and come back the next night. When I finally shared with people, they said to plead the blood of Jesus over you before you go to bed. That wasn't working. I would be scared my eyes were in bulk. God showed me the snakes couldn't harm me because they would only get close enough to bring fear. When I realized God was right, those dreadful nights vanished.

Doctors Visits

Doctor Providing What
I Don't Want

B y the time of the second visit, things seem to be looking better. At least I thought. Today will be different, the doctor added another medicine. Here's what is troubling, the extra medicine was the medicine used to dope up myself. Now I'm saying in my heart, "no doctor, not ready for this one." "What has changed since the last visit?" Would I know if I am worse? What's going on here? Am I in my right frame of mind?"

Sure, I had some fine days and emotional days, but not to be given this med. I was feeling better before this visit. I believe God has stepped in, but yet this med. "Lord Jesus!" I'm just looking at the doctor, wanted to say, "Wait a minute, what happened?" My heart was saying, "No, no, no; let's review this one." I could see; his determination for me to received this new medicine.

All of a sudden, "I refuse to let this pull me down." I wasn't planning on losing the peace or joy that returned to me. I will take this prescription and have it filled, "not planning on using it, not now," no way, and hoping it won't be soon. Maybe the doctor sees something and not telling me. Whatever it may be, I am determined to go through this stage of using drugs to dope up. "Give me, a break here; there isn't any more rushing here and not planning on leaving this world before the time!" Everything else was good; blood pressure was up probably and more up now. Wait a minute, why the nurse and staff were being over-emotional. I noticed when I came in this morning; the staff was looking at me. The doctor team had that sorrowful look on their face; they knew I would receive this prescription today.

Yep, they knew, but here's what they need to do, keep all of their sorrow to themselves. I don't need this, not here. I made the appointment, walked through those doors with my head lifted. I knew everyone was watching me, and I didn't care. In my mind, and my walk telling them I'm not going to be like everyone else in here. That's not me, and I Am a fighter. Now, this is my life, and I'm not throwing in the towel. "Get behind me," Satan. You can't have my day. I finally began to understand. "It wasn't God," that was trying to kill me. "It was the devil!" Plotting, scheming, and trying to shame me; I'm coming from up under this Lupus. "I will not stay in this confinement."

Doctor Is Clever and Watching

I've learned the doctor was watching everything I say and my movements. Before the doctor was making his plan concerning the visit, God already knew his plan. It was God who informed me on the office visit. One test, trying to see how easily I get confused. Remember, Lupus has its way with the mind. Once I notice, I refuse to let anything get next to me. I took a deep breath to help relax my body.

My appearance was important." God has already informed me, "whenever there is any doctor appointment, get up early to pray before you go." You see, the effectual fervent prayer of a righteous man [or woman] availeth much. That's me; the enemy was scheming like he's always done. God said to pray. That prayer was for me. I needed to be in the doctor's office in my right mind.

During the praying, I always ask God to help me, strengthen me, and guard my mind, mouth, and heart. I ask God to give me wisdom and stay with me. To help get me through this day, the day of the office visit. Listen, every time, "I closed the door, in the moment I turned around," I raised my hand up and said Thank you, Jesus.' A smile came immediately on my face, and before I could push the other door open to go across the waiting room, joy would feel in my heart. Their looks didn't bother me anymore, and they were amazed. "I refuse to give my day away." "Refuse to be sad." Worry was an enemy; "God doesn't worry; he doesn't have any need to. So why shall I worry and become stressed out? Somewhere along the journey, I've learned to be determined in everything I do.

Keeping an Open
Line Between
God and Yourself

The Importance of Prayer

Prayer is vital to our lives. Its' during learning how to pray that you develop your relationship with God. Prayer deals with open communication between you and God. Prayer is where the Father waits on you to enter; he already knows before you come. God will never force you to pray. During learning how to pray that your spiritual lessons start. God himself wants to breathe upon you. He wants to instruct you, to teach you, to train you. He will use the Holy Spirit through this process. God's hands are upon you, this day to restore you. Now God is waiting on you to come to him; he has the perfect peace and strength you need. Understand that because God had established his plan for you, your part is to follow through.

Sharing time: Holy Spirit taught me, when I come to the Lord in prayer, come with my faith, believe before I approach God. To reach God, I have to go through Jesus. The following ways develop needed for maturity and growth:

- spending time in his words
- studying his words
- reading his word
- meditating in his word

- praying his word
- becoming his word
- watching what you say and what you do

To walk upright before Him, understand he is my rewarder and mediator. To walk in obedience to him, act on the word, be quick to repent and forgive. Watch what you let into your spirit because your body is the temple of God, the Holy Spirit lives in you, and He is holy. To put your complete trust in God and don't allow anyone to control you. Live a lifestyle of holiness.

The word of God tells us God is holy, and we are holy. God lavished his love on us; we need to lavish our love on him. Don't mummer, complain, gossip; trust God, for He is your source, your strength, and cares about everything concerning you. Daily surrendering to him. Always remember God is a jealous God, and to have any other gods. Don't forget about the blood of Jesus. The blood of Jesus covers and wash us, the word of God cleanses us, and the Word is God himself.

The Holy Spirit teaches trains, leads, guides, comforter, and a counselor. The Holy Spirit tells us what the Father says and speaks only the truth because he comes from our Father. Prayer is essential. Prayer requires your faith in action. In Hebrews 11:6, King James Version, But without faith it is impossible to please him: for he that cometh to God must believe that he is and that he is a rewarder of them that diligently seek him.

Prayer helps develop you; God weighs our heart, he sees the heart, he knows whether or not you are diligently seeking him. What makes prayer powerful is the seeker, the ones who spend time learning God, a repentance heart, a renewed mind, a praiser, and a worshiper. In Psalm 51:10 King James Version, Create in me a clean heart, O God; and renew a right spirit within me. Especially when you think you know how to pray, and one day, there is the truth, you don't know how to pray. I am sure anyone can say, Father, Thank You Lord, and Hallelujah. Have you ever thought about how God has a pattern of prayer? Think about this, if Jesus' disciples ask Jesus to teach them how to pray, what about your own prayer life? How often do you pray? To whom do you pray? What is Jesus saying about your prayer life?

See, I was ashamed of my prayer life. In my heart, I believe I was praying to God, and he was listening. First of all, I had to ask God to forgive me and then ask myself to forgive me. I was humiliated; I ask God to teach me how to pray. I had to learn who the Holy Spirit was, where He came from, and how long I need to pray. Why did I have to pray? With God being God, why was prayer important? One word, *relationship*. Prayer is more than you sharing; it is God sharing himself. Did you not know, God has a great sense of humor? Through prayer, "I learn about his sense of humor; through prayer, I understand how he values praise and loves for us to minister to him, to worship him.

He will instruct the Holy Spirit to teach you to pray. Your life will change for the better simply because you're going to walk in obedience to the Father. So don't look at it like I'm leaving you hanging; it's yours for the asking. Understand, God established this way for you to come before Him, and the Holy Spirit is your leader through this journey. The Holy Spirit just expresses to give you some prayer pointer. There will be other scriptures of prayer following the Holy Spirit. (Prayer of Salvation in the back of the book). Remember, how do you know if you belong to God? Because you have the Holy Spirit is living inside of you.

Prayer Pointers

Prayer Pointer 1: Pattern of Prayer (Matthew 6:9 - 13)

Prayer Pointer 2: Asking in prayer and forgive (Mark 11:24 - 25 New Living Translation)

Prayer Pointer 3: Reminder (who you are) and how to enter (Psalm 100)

Prayer Pointer 4: Come through the right way, through the right person (John 14:6)

Prayer Pointer 5: Don't be in a hurry to pray, listen and hear, before you pray

Prayer Pointer 6: There is a place for praise, thanksgiving, and worship (Psalm 100)

Prayer Pointer 7: There is a time for you to minister unto the Holy Spirit, and He will minister unto you.

Prayer Pointer 8: Invite the Holy Spirit In, he is such a gentleman and never forces himself in any way.

Prayer Pointer 9: Be a good steward of the Word of God, search the scripture, and you will find Him.

Prayer Pointer 10: Don't forget to pray for others; what you make happen for one God will make happen for you. (We do this by praying or by what God is speaking to you to do).

Father, in the name of Jesus, I pray these prayer pointers penetrate their heart and mind. I ask You forgive them of their sins and open their eyes of understanding as you show them how to pray, and I pray they won't neglect prayer.

Repeat this after me: Lord teach me how to pray, in Jesus' name. Amen.

I just brought you into an agreement with God's word, now you do your part, and the Holy Spirit is willing to do His part.

Calling Those Things
Into Existence

God instructed me to lay my hands on things and speak to them in Jesus' name, and while speaking, tell it what I need to happen, and it will happen. When you called in what you need to take place, you have to believe it will happen, and this is an area where doubt must not occur. Laying on of hands is a spiritual transformation. For every work you do, you must have a clean heart and a pure heart. (As it is written, I have made thee a father of many nations,) before him whom he believed, even God, who quickeneth the dead, and calleth those things which be not as though they were (Romans 4:17 King James Version). Notice I underlined a specific portion of the scripture. God was speaking this to Abraham, and because Abraham has this, we also have the right to call those things into being.

Let's go to another scripture: (John 1:3 King James Version), All things were made by him: and without him was not any thing that was made. (Him in this scripture is God). Lets' define the word thing: an object or entity not precisely designated or capable of being designated; a separate and distinct individual quality, fact, idea, or usually entity; the concrete entity as distinguished from its appearances; a spatial entity; state of affairs in general or within a specified or implied sphere; whatever may be possessed or owned or be the object of a right, an article of clothing; equipment or utensils especially for a particular purpose; Deed, Act, accomplishment, detail, point; a spoken or written observation or point. ("Thing," Merriam-Webster.com Dictionary)

Since we define the word thing, let's identify. God taught me to lay hands on things; everything in the doctor's office was a thing: blood pressure machine, stethoscope, pulse oximeter, reflex hammer, tongue depressors, swabs. All doctors have different types of equipment. When I look around the room, I saw the blood pressure machine, wondering how I will lay my hands on this machine. The nurse said, "Ms. Morrow, need you to hold the blood pressure machine because the part which allowed the device to stand has been broken. If you hold it up like this, it will work fine." I am excited because God informed me to lay hands on the equipment. Do you see it: God told me to lay hands, the nurse asked me to hold the blood pressure machine up, which is equipment, and now it was my turn to carry out the order.

What did I say? In the name of Jesus, I command this blood pressure machine to give me a good reading. I command my pressure to line up with the word of God, and when you go down, you cannot go down too fast, which makes me sick from it, a perfect reading in the name of Jesus. The doctor couldn't believe I have a good blood pressure reading, but I could.

God said that spiritual connection would work without you putting your hand on someone. Example: Father, in the name of Jesus, let this doctor knows how to talk with me give me favor with him and you. During this time, my arm stretched out toward the direction the office was. Do you know, I just set up the doctor's visit? The doctor was careful in choosing his words.

There will be lessons to learn when you walk your way out of your Lupus or any problems. The Holy Spirit taught me: Pray before you go; cover yourself with the blood of Jesus, bind what you need to stop from happening, and loose what you need to take place, Be thankful unto the Lord with a grateful heart; Praise Him for what he had done and what he's going to perform for you, Tell yourself it is well in your soul, Refuse to be sick and refuse to doubt and give the devil no place in your life. Take authority over negative and idle words. If you go to the doctor and everything is not correct, don't believe the devil's lie. Good words don't lie, and God doesn't lie. Why? Because God is the word. You keep trusting in God, keep believing for the manifestation of your healing, keeping calling your healed, you'll be whole. Your healing will manifest; stay with God, obey his voice, learn from him, meditate in God's word.

Casting My Cares Upon the Lord

In going through with Lupus, I found out it was absolutely better to get rid of problems. Many days after studying God's word, I came upon this one: Cast thy burden upon the LORD, and he shall sustain thee: he shall never suffer the righteous to be moved (Psalms 55:22 King James Version) also In (1 Peters 5:7 King James Version) Casting all your care upon him; for he careth for you. In (Matthew 11:28 King James Version), Come unto me, all that labour and are heavy laden, and I will give you rest.

When I gave Jesus my heart and became save, born-again, I immediately became the righteousness of God. There was nothing I did but receive my salvation, born-again, my new life, my true identity in Christ Jesus. I love it when I can go to God's throne room and get rid of things, the care of this world, people junks, anything that offends me, worrying me. I can leave it at his feet and have the faith he will handle it. I need to believe this before I go into the throne room, operating in doubt not going to solve the problem. It takes our faith.

Tell God everything about the problem, search your heart because God will not be deceived. He already knows your heart before you go into the throne room. God is all-knowing.

There was a lesson for me to learn, called You Just Can't Tell God On Other Peoples Without Sharing You, and you will be the first person to talk about you and then the person you have problems with. It will cause you to view things differently because you will see it through the eyes of God.

Holding God Accountable In Remembrance of His Word

There will be times when God will tell you some things, and you are waiting on God to come through with what he promised. God is faithful unto his words. In (Isaiah 43:26 King James Version), Put me in remembrance: let us plead together; declare thou, that thou mayest be justified. I take this promise seriously because I can take God to his holy written words and say it boldly, You said. God does not lie, He is faithful to His word, God honors His word, God moves on His Word, the Word of God is God Himself. Don't be scared to use His word. Use your faith to remind God of what he said to you.

Example One: Healing

God, you said, you will heal me: 1 Peter 2:24 King James Version, Who his own self bare our sins in his own body on the tree, that we being dead to sins, should live unto righteousness: by whose stripes ye were healed. Those are your holy written words, not mine, and if you don't come through, that makes you a liar, and your word says. God is not a man, that he should not lie; neither the son of man, that he should repent: hath he said (now that you God) and shall not do it? Hath he spoken, and shall he not make it good? (Numbers 23:19 King James version).

Example Two: Find several scriptures on different things to use.

God, you said: Beloved, I wish above all things that thou mayest prosper and be in health, even as thy soul prospereth. (3 John 2 King James Version)

God, you said: Now unto him that is able to do exceeding abundantly above all that we ask or think, according to the power that worketh in us, to him be glory in the church by Christ Jesus throughout all ages, world without end. Amen (Ephesians 3:20-21 King James version)

God, you said: Thou will keep him in perfect peace, whose mind is stayed on thee: because he trusted in thee. (Isaiah 26:3 King James Version)

God, you said: The steps of a good man are ordered by the Lord: and he delighteth in his way. (Psalm 37:23 King James Version).

God, you said: In all thy ways acknowledge Him, and he shall direct thy paths. (Proverbs 3:6 King James Version)

God you said, The eyes of the LORD are in every place, Keeping watch on the evil and the good (Proverbs 15:3 New King James Version).

God, you said: A merry heart makes a cheerful countenance, But by sorrow of the heart the spirit is broken (Proverbs 15:13 New Kings James Version)

God, you said: Though I walk in the midst of trouble, You will revive me: You will stretch out Your hand Against the wrath of my enemies (Psalm 138:7 New King James Version)

God, you said: If you abide in me, and my words abide in you, ye shall ask what ye will, and it shall be done unto you (John 15:7 King James Version).

God, you said: The blessing of the LORD, it maketh rich, and he added no sorrow with it (Proverbs 10:22 King James Version).

God, you said: And the Lord shall make thee the head, and not the tail; and thou shalt be above only, and thou shalt not be beneath; if that thou hearken unto the commandments of the Lord thy God, which I command thee this day, to observe and to do them (Deuteronomy 28:13 King James Version).

God, you said: But He answered and said, "It is written: Man shall not live by bread alone, but by every word that proceedeth out of the mouth of God." (Matthew 4:4 King James Version)

God, you said: And we know that in all things God works for the good of those who love him, who have been called according to his purpose. (Romans 8:28 New International Version).

"Don't forget, God has given us promises to stand on, to use. Also, God is the Word of God."

Laying Up Treasures

In the darkest moment of my life, death was supposed to occur or might not happen. I knew there was a better way than for me to take my life. I believe God was going to do what I had already asked of him if that time occurred. No parents, sister, brother, or child wanted to hear their loved one talk about death. I knew my family was going to say she was not going anywhere before God's timing. It's not my desire to live in a world, not at myself laying flat on my back for years. No, that's a family that doesn't want to let go. I needed them to let go and live their lives in the fullness of God. I used to struggle with the ideal of dying but in the word of God: "For to me to live is Christ, and to die is gain." (Philippians 1:21 King James Version) God was saying while I am living my life for Christ now, but by any circumstances, I should die, Debbie will live again but on the other side and on that side there is no sickness there, and no suffering, no worry, but peace, love, and joy. The other side was to be home with Jesus. I knew God would honor his words, so I began to search for them until I believed in my heart it was the right one to hold him accountable.

During those moments of searching the scriptures, I came upon the one talking about laying up treasures. There is a place within heaven, where prayers are stored up and here the marvelous thing about it. Can't nobody claim yours for you. I knew if the day ever came, then I was definitely going to need some help. After replaying everything in my mind of the horrible ordeal that was to take place in my life. There was going to be no way my family was going to make the decision for me when they needed to. I know, the doctor could have given me papers to sign, but in my heart, it was better for God to intervene. For me, it was prayers that were already prayed by me, designed to come to pass whenever I'm in need. The doctor stated how strenuously and probably just living in the living land, not knowing anyone or myself. I had to act upon the word of God. In (Matthew 6:19-21 King James Version), Lay not up for yourselves treasures upon earth, where moth and rust doth corrupt, and where thieves break through and steal: But lay up for yourselves treasures in heaven, where neither moth nor rust doth corrupt, and where thieves do not break through nor steal: For where your treasure is, there will your heart be also.

I needed this prayer to reach heaven and be on demand. Everything the doctor said that probably will happen to me, I pray to God about it. I realize when people are sick and their loved one watches them going through, it is not easy for the one whos' sick or the loved ones. I didn't want to put my family through any of the hurt. I believe the decision should be mine to make, not my family.

Prayer

By Minister Debbie Hollins

Father, in the name of Jesus, that name which is above all other's names and everything. I know that you can, and I know that you will answer my petition. I know you as a forgiving God. I ask you to forgive me of all of my sins, and I forgive those who trespass against me, and I pray if I trespass against anyone, they forgive me of my trespasses. I ask you to lead me not into temptation but to deliver me from all evil and harm. You are God Almighty and wonderful, and excellent is your name. Heaven and earth may pass away, but your name is everlasting. You are an amazing, unique, powerful, loving, and merciful God. You specialized in things that are impossible to men.

My Strong Tower, You are faithful to your words, and you watch over your word. I need you to honor your holy written words. I know you know all about this situation. I need you to fix it for me, Jesus. When I'm flat on my back, can't eat, eyes fix one way, jumping in bed, drooling from my mouth, wearing pampers, not knowing who I am and my family. I want you to roll back the ceiling, let my eyes look one way straight up, just like I'm looking into heaven. Father, you know my heart. It's between you and me and no one else. I'll be saying here am I, Lord. Here I am. Lord, you know what I need. I expect you to fix it in Jesus' name, Amen.

I am telling God don't leave me here in this place like this, I'll want to be home with him than to be here in that kind of shape, not in my right mind, just living in the land of the living. Just bring me home now.

Watch Your Words

Words Can Captive Your Soul

The Holy Spirit was teaching me and telling me to watch what I say, and how I respond to the words I hear. Once you release it, it will come to pass. We sow what we reap. Kindness begets kindness. In other words, if I need kindness then let kindness come from the mouth. If I want bad things, then let bad words come from my mouth. I learn to stop being negative and stop using negative words over myself and others. I found it hard to stop talking the way I've been talking for years. I never wanted to speak curses upon anyone, or have evil thinking of anyone. In reality, I had to get help, especially if this helped the healing process. Why not ask God? This is the scripture I found and I asked Him and he came through for me. In Psalm 141:3 King James Version: Set a watch, O Lord, before my mouth; keep the door of my lips. When I couldn't find positive words to say, I closed my mouth, here's the other one: Thou art snared with the words of thy mouth, thou are taken with the words of thy mouth (Proverbs 6:2 King James Version)

Now if you live for the Lord, then you know to pick good words to speak over yourself and others. Evil words, bad words, hateful words, slander words, come to cut you, pull you down, stop you from producing, and excel in your walk with the Lord. I had to ask God to help me in that area. My words are important for my maturity in the Lord, and my life. That naughty tongue, that impure thought, wicked ways, can not be if I am going to be an Ambassador for the Lord. Everything I had and had to change had to be transformed. Things were new for me, but it still was going to be God's way, or keep on going around in circles wondering why, and staying in the process longer. All I ever had to do was to simply embrace the journey and master it. God wanted me to fully be aware of my mouth, my tongue. Lesson learned the power of life and death in our tongue, and our words can reach, snare, capture and hold us hostage.

God Provides Encouragement

There is nothing like the Father's encouragement. God loves us so much, even to eternity. Days when I am at the lowest, God brings encouragement to me. It didn't matter whether my head was down or looking lost. God's encouragement provided hope and strength for my soul. Remember, God's ways are not our ways. God uses a song to minister into my heart. Every time I went to church, whether it was a church service or singing event, God reaches out to me, making sure He has my attention. What do I mean? The song was pulling me into it, and I began to lean toward the individual singing the song; that song would touch my heart. All of a sudden, the person would say before and during the song. I don't know who this song is for, but I know you are in this place; God loves you that much; just let the song ministered to your heart. Suddenly, I am listening to the song. If You Just Hold Out, by Rev. C.L. Franklin. It was this part of the song that captured my attention.

Here's some of the words that gave me encouragement:
If you just hold out until tomorrow, if you just keep the faith through the night;
If you just hold out until tomorrow, everything will be alright

"God's encouraging message was: Hold on, to keep the faith. Keep your faith, Debbie, through the night. If I don't come back to reclaim my church, then you know you can make it through another day. Why? "Because the next day, Debbie, you will be alright; hold on; keep your faith; don't turn loose; I still need for you to hold on, hold on." "I told the Lord, Okay, I will make it."

There were some days where the song didn't do anything for me. I was so down, there I am sitting in church, tears running down my face, just in a fog. I'm up, but Lord Jesus, you only know can't even put it in words, Jesus, this thing is just overwhelming. The lady was singing the song, and I mean singing the song. Suddenly, the lady starts pleading, talking, and speaking in a way she had my attention. I don't know you, lady, if you can just hold on, hold on, you will be okay, but you have to hold on, don't give in to what you are going through, what you are feeling but somehow find the faith, size of a mustard seed that all you need and know that God loves you, he's here, all you have to do is to reach out. Suddenly, the song started to minister to me, and yes, I cried, but this time the cry was different. It broke all of that weary frustration from off of me. "Hallelujah!" The lady who sang the song was ministering unto me, and because of the anointing on the song, things left from me, my breakthrough for that day were there. "To God be the Glory!"

Speaking Encouraging
Words Over Myself

Not only did God provide encouragement for me, I learned through the Holy Spirit that in order for me to rise within my confinement of Lupus, but I also had to get rid of the clothes of Lupus. Every day when I dressed myself, Lupus was dressing before I could stand on the floor. Every day I had to remind myself I am valuable. Everyday I look at myself in the mirror, standing there not liking myself, feeling disgusted with what I became. Had to turn the hurt and the way I see myself around.

My talk to myself:
I am Wonderful and Fearfully Made
I am God Masterpiece
I am Valuable
I am Loveable
I am Unique
I am One of a Kind
I am Strong
I am Courageous

I am Peculiar
I am Acceptable
I am Beautiful
I am Peaceful
I am Special
I have a Sound Mind
I have Strength for the day
I have Peace, Love, Joy
I am Royalty
I am in the Beloved Kingdom

The Three Essence Qualities

The Praise Carrier

I am not going to talk about what praise does to the enemy or how praise strengthens you. God wants you to fully understand; he made you for his glory and all praise due to him.

The praises coming from my heart through the doors of my lips shall always be admirable praise. God knows the heart of his children. Our praise is offered up with the sincerity of pure heart, which draws the heart of the Father. His attention toward you is joyful and lovable. Let's define admirable: According to Merriam-Webster.com Dictionary, Admirable is deserving the highest esteem: excellent; obsolete: exciting wonder: surprising. Synonyms of admirable: applaudable, commendable, creditable, estimable, laudable, meritorious, praiseworthy. When you are a true praise carrier, you excite God's heart. It moves him to look at you. When you are one with the praise, and the praise becomes one with the Father, it changes the atmosphere. "Why!" Praise is powerful and draws one to the Father.

"The Father stands, in awe of the praise. God inhabits praise." Let define the word inhabit: according to Merriam- Webster Dictionary says, inhabits to occupy as a place of settled residence or habitat: live in. To be present in or occupy in any manner or form.

Listen, there are times when I am the praise carrier. It moves God. He enjoys the praise, lending over-excitement about the praise. I picture God smiling and laughing and embracing the praise of what it truly is. Praise from my heart to the heart of the Father that continually causes breathtaking powerful unique fragrance of the Father's essence. God loved to be lavish in praise. Every day we live should be a day of praise to the Father. How many times a day? as much as you can. I challenge you to be "The Praise Carrier."

Scripture Reference
But thou art holy, O thou that inhabitest the praises of Israel (Psalm 22:3 King James Version).

But you are a chosen people, a royal priesthood, a holy nation, God's special possession, that you may declare the praises of him who called you out of darkness into his wonderful light (1 Peter 2:9 New International Version).

The Worshiper Experiences

Everyone who is called by my name, when I have created for my glory; I have formed him yes, I have made him (Isaiah 43:7 King James Version). God looks for his own, he seeks a worshipper. Worship is a spiritual oneness between the worshiper and God. When I surrender myself to Him, it becomes more personal. Everything I am connected with God. My heart, soul, body, mind, and spirit is never left out. There is an outward reaction to worship. The countenance changes, crying occurs, hands lifted up. You can find yourself saying "Yes Lord, not my will Lord, but thy will be done in me." I'm in His presence, standing in awe of his beauty. I am standing before majesty, I'm in the place where reverence, honor, glory, the oneness. The bond of perfectness in the midst of God splendor. I recognize the King of Glory is there, my heart yearns in His presence, my attention on the creator, the lover of my soul. It's deep calling for deep, it's breathtaking.

True worship is beyond praise, my praise and thanksgiving prepare me to enter in. The love, assurance and acceptance is there. Reaching, embracing an awesome Lord. "No connection", there is no worship. Worship draws also causes you to look at yourself. O come, let us worship and bow down: let us kneel before the Lord our maker (Psalm 95:6 King James Version). See whether I'm in service or home I bow down. Worship is spontaneously done with the whole heart. There is no place for waiver. Worship is the essence to why I'm there. See, worship is sacred unto God. Worship is real, truth, only for God and no one else. I find myself drawing unto Him, and He's drawing unto me. Spiritual things happen in worship. I can't sacrifice Jesus, he's already been sacrificed, so I offer myself completely to him. My sacrifice is my body from my head to my toes and from the inward part of the body. Worship is not hard, it requires you to surrender to the Father; don't think, don't perform, just do it.

"To God be the Glory!"

Scripture

"Yet a time is coming and has now come when the true worshipers will worship the Father in the Spirit and in truth, for they are the kind of worshipers the Father seeks. God is spirit, and his worshipers must worship in the Spirit and in truth." (John 4:23-24 New International Version)

"Give unto the LORD the glory due unto his name; worship the LORD in the beauty of holiness." (Psalm 29:2 King James Version)

The Encourager

I found, when I become an encourager, not only does it help the one who receives it, it also helps the one who releases it. The encouragement comes to build you up. Whether to strengthen or motivate you. It's never used to hinder, block, stop or harm anyone. Whether it's an encouraging word from the Lord or someone is singing an inspirational song, or you providing encouraging words. Encouragement always draws. Let your encouragement be mighty in the land. Take the initiative to pour into someone's life to help make their life better by turning around with your words.

I found, when I encourage them, I gain their attention. Your encouragement should be powerful enough that it touches their heart. Let your words of encouragement glorify God. Your encouragement from your heart shapes an individual's life journey and success. Will you be one, and then after the brought encouragement, step back and look, you'll be the witness to what you have actually spoken from your heart through your mouth reflecting the person spoken unto.

Scripture Reference

But encourage one another daily, as long as it is called "Today," so that none of you may be hardened by sin's deceitfulness (Hebrews 3:13 New International Version)

The lesson learned: I had to please God, not man. I'm in God's Kingdom. God truly sees things different from us. Learn God, know God, study God; causes you to develop your relationship with Him. One thing I know, God loves for me to praise him for who he is, and for what he has already done. During prayer, you will find me loving on him, praising him. I don't mind offering up praise, thanksgiving, and worship to an amazing Father.

In All Thy Getting Get Understanding

Knowledge is Power

You need to catch on to reality, the truth of the matter. You are in a fight, but turn your fight over to the Lord, and allow Him to fight that battle of Lupus for you, it is called Walking Your Way Out Through the Word of God. Knowledge is Power. In all thy getting you attain understanding. Simply stated, "God wants you heal, whole, and delivered from LUPUS." Remember, the thief (the enemy, the devil) comes to kill, steal, and destroy. For me, it's a new day now. My fight is back, and I will not be denied what belongs to me. The LORD is my light and my salvation; whom shall I fear? The LORD is the strength of my life, of whom shall I be afraid? (Psalm 27:1 King James Version). No longer scared of the enemy. I fear God, not man, nor the enemy. Reality had to return unto me, and my peace returned; it is God's peace we need. In Philippians 4:7 NIV: And the peace of God, which transcends all understanding, will guard your hearts and minds in Christ Jesus.

Let me break this down. God is not the one who brings confusion to our hearts and minds. If you deal with uncertainty, you're doubtful, in a daze, not thinking clearly, more easily distracted. Now you find yourself being pulled, where you have feelings of uneasiness, heaviness, confusion that's from the enemy, not God.

When we talk about the peace of God, there is peace within you that can cause calmness to settle deep down within, the knowing part inside you, or feel a release from something. Still, it's a good release and no more pressure, you know, without any doubt it had to be God in the midst of you moving on your behalf even when you didn't see it, but it moves. You're relaxed, calm, you've found pleasure, not pain from your hurt, and indeed not confusion. God gives us peace and his love.

Many are the afflictions of the righteous: but the LORD delivereth him out of them all. Now, what is afflictions, accordingly Merriam-Webster 1828 Dictionary, afflictions are:

- A cause of persistent pain or distress.
- Great suffering.
- The state of being afflicted by some things that causes suffering.

Here are the synonyms: agony, anguish, distress, excruciation, hurt, misery, pain, rack, straits, torment, torture, travail, tribulation, woe. This sickness was coming against my health. Some days I didn't know what to think, but God is faithful to His Words, his promises. Everything within me lets me know God is on my side; you will not die, you will live, you will be alright, but you must continually endure the process to see it to the end. God is with you! Let's back this up with the Word of God. What shall we then say to these things? If God is for us, who can be against us? (Romans 8:31 King James Version).

I shall not die, but live, and declare the works of the Lord (Psalm 118:17 King James Version). Let's break it down: I am not going anywhere before my time. God has work for me to do. God is preparing me for his work, and souls need to be delivered! Is it your soul? Understand this; if you feel bad, tired, upset, lonely, God has a word for it. The problem was, fear was driving me, holding me back. God being my Abba Father, the Holy Spirit taught me about fear.

Fear has torment, it comes to rob you of everything you have, even the relationship with God. God desires to keep us in perfect peace; our mind and focus need to be on him. The secret is to abide in God. For when we abide in God, there is everything we need for our spiritual journey. The Father does provide for us, it's the Father who wants you heal, whole, save, and deliver. The enemy blocks our pathway, and God will use what the enemy means for our bad, make it work for our good. Trust the Father's plans. It will be God who brings you through! Praise the LORD, who is my rock. He trains my hands for war and gives my fingers skill for battle [Psalm 144:1 King James Version]. Let me tell you, God will have the Holy Spirit to train you how to fight, His way, not your way, but His way. Listen: There is a way which seemeth right unto man, but the end thereof are the ways of death (Proverbs 14:12 King James Version). See, we all need the ways of God to live.

The rock is solid and not ever going to break; the rock is Jesus built upon the solid ground of the Word of God. For the word of God is alive and active. Sharper than any double-edged sword, it penetrates even to dividing soul and spirit, joints and marrow; it judges the thoughts and attitudes of the heart [Hebrews 4:12 New International Version].

Let me go back to talk about the Abba Father briefly. He is the one who nourishes you, wipes your eyes when you cry. He tells you, there is no need for you to cry because Abba Father is here. The one who comforts you and assures you everything is going to be alright. He's the one that wraps his loving arms around you, cheering you along your way. He's the one you get to know, Don't you understand, "God will move the mountain for you, one scripture says, God will leap over walls for us." God doesn't want you down, because he's there waiting on you to trust him with your life. He wants you to share your day with him, and God wants to share with you things only he can know that will amaze you. "It's God's will for me to live and spend time with him; he's the lover of our soul; think about it."

Here's how I know! And the LORD said unto Satan, From whence comest thou? And Satan answered the LORD, and said, From going to and fro in the earth, and from walking up and down in it (Job 2:2 King James Bible). Satan looks to see who he thinks you can take out or plots to take people out of the world by making them think God is trying to kill them when it was Satan. Those blows, stings, lies, sickness, the let downs, people talking about you, or you just can't pull yourself together, it was the effect of Satan snares, his plots and tricks, that's who he is. God is all-powerful and all-knowing and forgiving.

Now, who does he think he is? My life belongs to God, not him. Debbie doesn't follow him and obeys him. Is he not my Lord? "NO". God always warns his children, and the warning comes before destruction. You have to hear and listen. It's the Holy Spirit's job to teach and train us. I'm talking to the born-again believers. You have the spirit of God inside of you. If you are not God's children, he still will heal you as well. Why? Because God is not a respectable person. In Acts 10:34, Then Peter, having opened his mouth, and said, Of a truth I perceive that God is no respecter of persons: [King James Bible]the New International Version reads: Then Peter began to speak: "I now realize how true it that God does not show favoritism. Here's the reality, if you don't make Him (GOD), Lord in your life you will miss the wonderful benefits God has for His children living with him especially when this corrupt world ends, you want to see His throne room to see heaven.

Let's be perfectly clear, my fight is back, and my stance is back. In other words, there's no need to run from the enemy. The enemy works in the unseen realm, specializing in making you think that God and someone else has violated you. In reality, the enemy, the devil, the accuser of the brethren, in disguise laying dominate. The enemy lays silently unto the time to show up and move out toward you, just waiting on someone to use, simply because he can never be at the same place at the same time, only God because God is Omnipresence. The enemy has to find someone to use to do his work, God doesn't, and if God chose to bring someone in your path, it's never to shame you, but at times will cause you to look at your mistake, but God forgives us despite what we do. Did you catch all of those things the enemy does? "Yes, the enemy comes to deceive you, to turn your heart away from God."

The Truth

The enemy had a plan of taking my life, but God wasn't allowing the enemy to end my life. Not before the time and he would never be the one to end my life! Sometimes I often stated the enemy was dumb. Why? He always tried, tried, and tried, but all God had to do was to show up. "In my overdrive, emotional moments" the devil, the accuser of the brethren, "would do absurd things." No matter how hard the enemy tries to bring death, my heavenly Father intervenes. "Yes," the plan of sickness through SLE had a purpose, but I am purpose, so because of my purpose, the enemy had to plot, scheme, and try to turn my heart away from God. Everything, the enemy, Satan did, God turned it all around and got the Glory. Hear me, from everything which it caused me, Debbie was tremendously blessed by it.

The journey became a spiritual journey. You thought the enemy who fell from God's grace would know he and his army couldn't stop God's purpose. The enemy's job was to distract me from my God-given purpose. The enemy doesn't mind using anyone he can to stop the children of God from knowing their purpose. He looks for people to recruit for his kingdom. One of the devil's greatest tasks is to stop the born-again believer from knowing their true identity in Christ. "But, through my Lupus Journey, the Holy Spirit trained me, my stand is in the Lord.

For in Him we live and move and exist [that is, in Him, we actually have our being], as even some of your own poets have said, "for we also are his children" (Acts 17:28 Amplified Bible). Now the question has been asked. Who shall separate us from the love of Christ? Shall tribulation, or distress, or persecution, or famine, or nakedness, or peril, or sword?

As it is written, For thy sake we are killed all the day long; we are accounted as sheep for the slaughter. Nay, in all these things we are more than conquerors through him that loved us.

For I am persuaded, that neither death, nor life, nor angels, nor principalities, nor powers, nor things to come, nor height, nor depth, nor any other creature shall be able to separate us from the love of God, which is in Christ Jesus our Lord (Romans 8:35-39 King James Version). And let us say, Amen, you've just agreed with the Word of God.

Let us continue. "The enemy forgets," When the righteous cry [for help], the LORD hears And rescues them from all their distress and troubles (Psalm 34:17 Amplified Bible). The enemy loves to bring confusion and sift the knowledge of God from your heart. See, the adversary, the liar, pulls out things to stop you and keep you bound. He's a clever, little foe, trying to keep you out of the heavenly Kingdom of GOD. It was Satan's choice; he is a deceiver, don't keep falling prey to the enemy. Let's go to the Word of God. Whenever God speaks to us, through His Holy written words, and you see these three-letter words, You believe God; you have the authority to hold God accountable of His Word. What is the three-letter word? ALL, there is nothing that comes up short in ALL, nothing completely missing in ALL, ALL cannot be denied. All is a promised word given to you from God Himself.

Did you know or forget? "God took an oath to His word." Here's the other point, Satan doesn't want you to know the truth; the authority of the Word of God cuts things away from us we don't need. So, Satan uses his team to throw curve balls our way; but you've already more than conquerors. You give the command, and you make your declarations of declares and decrees. You'll not be under the enemy; the enemy is under your foot. One of the most significant abilities men and women always have is the authority to come within any circumstance, any situation, any dilemma, any valleys, any depression, any disease, and any sickness. We are not to stay bound; we get up, and we learn from our mistakes and press on, move on. Do you realize, Our knowledge of an Excellence Savior, the world greatness Redeemer, an Awesome Strong Tower, and a Brilliant Father, is on our side? God the Father is for you. He sees you. He knows you. Why? He called you for His very own. "Come On, pull yourself together, let's do it God's way. It requires you to lay down the cares of this world. To know your Abba Father loves you, and His love is never failing. He doesn't trick you into loving Him. Why? Because He is love. It's God in the beginning, in the middle, and in the ending of your life journey who loves you despite what you do."

Come from within your grief, sorrows, shame, hurt, distress, rejection, blows, mistrust, anger, the agony. Come to the Savior; he never left you; it was the enemy in disguise making you think, making you believe God stop loving you and caring for you, leaving you standing there alone. With all types of deception, lies, confusion, disgrace, who would do the terrible, horrific, appalling, dreadful, horrendous, intimidating, shocking ordeal. "Nobody," but Satan, the accuser of the brethren, that thief. Get angry at him, not God. How does God make a way out for his children? Evidence; There hath no temptation taken you but such as is common to man: but God is faithful, who will not suffer you to be tempted above all ye are able; but will with the temptation also make a way to escape, that ye may be able to bear it (1Corinthians 10:13 King James Version). Don't let the enemy lead and guide you. Let the Holy Spirit lead and guide you; that's what he does and will speak only the things from the Father.

Don't ever forget! Jesus is the Son of Man with purpose. Let's go to the Word. He that committeth sin is of the devil; for the devil sinneth from the beginning. For this purpose, the Son of Man was manifested, that he might destroy the works of the devil (1 John 3:8 King James Version). Let's look at the same bible verse in a different version. The one who practices sin [separating himself from God, and offending Him by acts of disobedience, indifference, or rebellion] is of the devil [and takes his inner character and moral values from him, not God]; for the devil has sinned and violated God's law from the beginning The Son of God appeared for this purpose, to destroy the works of the devil (1 John 3:8 Amplified Bible). One more, let this set this inside of you.

But you belong to God, my dear children. You have already won a victory over those people, because the Spirit who lives in you is greater than the Spirit who lives in the world (1 John 4:4 New Living Translation). Listen to this one (Luke 4:40 King James Version), Now when the sun was setting, all they that had any sick with divers diseases brought them unto him; and he laid his hands on every one of them, and healed them. Jesus laid his hands on them all, and he didn't separate people regarding healing.

Reaching Out

L upus is a disease; which affects your immune system. Your immune system has an important responsibility to protect your body from infections. Unfortunately, when your body has Lupus it seems like everything is off. "Why?" Because your immune system attacks your immune system. In other words, your white blood cells attack your red blood cells, and your red blood cells attack white blood cells.

For this reason, it appears there is a battle going on within and controlling the body physically and mentally. Some days seem normal, and some days are not normal. When those days, which are not normal, arrive, the flares up of Lupus make it unspeakable and unbearable. It's in those days you find your personality has shifted within another place of despair. You'll try, but it's not there; you become tired, touchy, withdrawn, feeling sorry, confused, and, yes, hopeless.

You lose your desire to be around other people, and it's in a way you don't know what's taken place. Next, you'll find yourself being pulled from the crowd of people, even your own family because this Lupus is driving you. Lupus moves into the stage of isolating yourself from everyone and everything that you love. You refuse to come out within the situation, and the problem is that trying to make you believe it's just no good or too late. "No," Jesus wants to know will be made whole. You can't use salvation as an excuse. Jesus wants you whole! Will you let Jesus heal you? Without knowing it, little by little, your fight is gone; you don't care to fight Lupus. At times your talk is silent, just looking to be by yourself. How can you do these things when there is no strength, no peace, no joy, no laughter, but pain and emptiness. You got to come out of living within the confinements of Lupus, those blows, and knockdowns.

"Aren't you tired of feeling that way?" "Aren't you tired of trying to express yourself to others when you know they don't understand?" You know this, but you have to make up your mind to stop living with the confinements of Lupus. Stop allowing Lupus to catch you. Stop allowing Lupus to pull you back into the place of loneliness. You might not be fighting Lupus, "But Lupus is fighting to keep you there in isolation against your will." Stop being the hostage to Lupus. Come on and take hold of your reality; Jesus is right here. He's your reason to come from within your confinements. Jesus is your reality! Will you be made whole? I'm not telling you to jump into a river, or harm yourself or stop taking your meds. Jesus wants to know, aren't you tired of living in pain, living in frustration. Don't you think it's time to live again?

Sweet Victory

T he moment my feet touched the floor, I knew this day was my day. You talk about knowing within my entire body. Everything within me was saying this is the day the Lord has made. I was determined there's nothing, no one or anything could take away what belongs to me today. The peace of God brought indwelling peace only God gives to us. In my heart, I was fully persuaded Lupus will not come back upon me again. The day of true rejoicing, the reassurance of God. There was no more uncertainty, lack of confidence, doubt, worry, confusion, or fear. I could finally embrace Jesus as my healer, deliver, the lover of my soul. The one who turns the bitter experiences into sweet experiences, the one who keeps his word and never lies.

And we know that in all things God works for the good of those who love him, who have been called according to his purpose (Romans 8:28 New International Version). This is the Lord's doing; it is marvellous in our eyes (Psalm 118:23 King James version). Today has already been established in heaven and on earth. Heaven declares Debbie Morrow completely healed from Systemic Lupus Erythematosus. I found no fault in God but the enemy. Hallelujah to the King of Glory! Who is this King of Glory? The Lord strong and mighty, the Lord mighty in battle (Psalm 24:8 King James Version). I am excited about what God is doing within me today. I can't wait to see my doctor and his staff when I walk through this morning's office doors. It will be God who releases me from their reports today. Debbie believes in the Report of the Lord. Get -thee- behind me, Satan. You have been exposed in more than one way. There's no stopping me now from believing in what God has done for me; sweet victory is mine today! Oh, what love, the Father has for me!

We finally made it to the doctor's office, and I practically jumped out of the car; I couldn't wait to go in. I took a deep breath and began to look at the building for the last time as I moved toward the door to go inside. No more of this place; these days are over with, praise the Lord. Suddenly, I stepped through those doors, looked around, refused to let anyone get next to me, walked straight to sign in, and was happy to sign my name. Taking my seat and hearing the nurse, "Debbie Morrow, are you here?" I hop up from the chair and start walking, saying, "Yes, I'm here." The nurse was looking at me, and I smiled. "Ms. Morrow, today you will see me, and I will inform the doctor. As you can see, we are swamped, and I am surprised the doctor is seeing you today instead of another day." Saying under my breath, "I'm not surprised; this day belongs to me."

The nurse, "Ms. Morrow, let's go into this room. "Okay." Tell me, how's everything has been? You appear to be looking fine, is there something peculiar that has been bothering you? Also, is it bothering you now?" "No! I'm fine, and nothing is bothering me." "Good, let's move on. Tell me about your swelling." "There is no swelling. "Yes, I can see there is none. What about before this visit? How was the swelling in your knees? Were there any other types of swelling in the joints?"

"As you can see, I'm fine, and since the last time here, I have hardly had any pain or swelling." "What about the hardly days? How often was hardly?" "Hardly ever." "Okay on these hardly ever days, what do you mean by hardly ever?" "I mean, yes, I had some, but there were not many of them. I barely had swelling, and I was hurting for a few days, and that's all." Okay, let's move on to check the blood pressure; of course, you will need to hold the machine tilted up." Okay, I am taking authority of this pressure in the name of Jesus, believing all is well. Blood pressure was all right. Nurse, okay, let's check your pressure again." The second blood pressure reading was fine, this time the nurse saying unh. Here I go, "Is there something wrong?" Nurse, "No, there appears to be nothing wrong. Let's check it again to make sure things are not off due to you holding the machine up." "Okay." In the third reading, a big smile is on my face. We are looking at each other; the nurse appears to be amazed. The doctor is calling her from the hallway. In my mind, saying this is rude, the doctor talking from the hallway. The nurse informs him my blood pressure is okay. The doctor asks for another reading to be taken. At this time, the nurse informed the doctor, she had already rechecked my pressure, and blood pressure was alright.

All of a sudden the doctor, asked the nurse to come and bring the file with her. Suddenly the doctor entered the room. "Hello Ms. Morrow, "I have read your file and it looks like everything is good. There wasn't anything wrong with your present exam today and looking back in the file from the last visit here, there weren't any problems." After carefully reviewing the file, I concluded there's no Lupus. When you came to see me, I took the other doctor's words and findings but didn't do my own test. If I had run my test, I could have found out early you didn't have Lupus, although the blood work from the Lupus Foundation showed Lupus, and now there's none." "So I don't have Lupus?" "There's no Lupus." Thank you."

Did you catch it? The doctor was trying to say I never had Lupus, but the primary evidence of the blood work proved him wrong. He had to rethink his finding because the people who specialize in Lupus did the blood work. The Lupus Foundation stated I had Lupus, and the first doctor's exams, plus blood work, prove Lupus. If there was no blood work by the specialists, the doctor could hold onto other possibilities. I never knew of any doctor treating people for a disease they don't have, especially for almost a year. I refused to have a discussion with the doctor or anyone else there. The enemy wasn't going to steal my joy anymore. All I wanted was the doctor's final report. That is why I can say, sweet victory. I believe most doctors don't believe in God healing anyone; they believe solely in the medical science of health.

The day I noticed I was feeling better was when it all started to turn around for me. The truth of the matter, God completely healed me of Lupus. I left the office and went straight to the bathroom and told the Lord thank you. I was excited. I wanted to scream out loud, "No more Lupus, Lupus free." I offer up praise and thanksgiving from the bathroom. The moment I stepped outside of the bathroom, people were staring at me. I said, "Lord, I know these people couldn't hear me praising You because it was down low." All of a sudden, I realized they heard me, but that was okay. "To God be the Glory."

I always thought, "God chasten me because of my behavior towards him. God recently shared, he didn't chasten me, but there were some things I needed to be broken from and during the most difficult times of Lupus." God decides when, where and if he disciplines his children. Yes, God chastens those whom he loved, but for me, he chose to test me. Be careful of what you ask of the Lord; I often pray Psalm 26:2, Examine me, O LORD, and try me; Test my mind and my heart. If there is anything within my heart and mind, I ask you to remove them from me. Show me the things I need to repent of, and I will repent. I need you daily in my life. Help me to bring you more glory, Lord. When you pray God's word, he does answer, and accepts our invitation.

Remember God has the original plans for your life. "Call unto me, and I will answer thee, and show thee great and mighty things, which thou knowest not (Jeremiah 33:3 King James Version)." What was my outcome? Completely heal, whole, and deliver from Lupus, Preacher, Praise and Worship Leader, Prayer Warrior, College Prayer Team, Author, and businesses I haven't possessed yet. Take away from this memoir, when you stay before the Lord, spending time in his presence, searching his word, believing in him, learning his ways, what he hates and what God loves, you can walk your way through your healing with the Word of God. God is for you; God is with you! God sees you, and God hears you. Amen, Sweet Victory!

Walking Your Way Through Your Healing With the Word of God

On your spiritual journey: Requires your faith, obedience to God. Stay faithful to God, in your moments of illness, weakness, and discouraging moments the Holy Spirit will tell you what the Father is speaking about the situation and how to properly deal with your situation. Walking your way through your healing deals with you being in the Word of God daily. Just follow the plan, God has established. This is between you and God. Honor him, get to know him, and the Holy Spirit.

The Process to Your Healing

- Ask the Lord to help you and teach you how to pray.
- Forgive yourself (Example: Say, to yourself, I'm sorry for allowing you to go through with all of this hurt, shame, and pain, for saying things I did not have any right to speak and not for guarding my mind, and heart. I release you from all wrongdoing, speaking negative words from this day forward Spirit of Truth to operate in my life from this moment on, in Jesus Name, Amen.
- Walk-in Forgiveness be quick to forgive others. Whether it's intentional or not. Forgiveness helps your healing process.
- Ask the Lord to create in you a clean heart (Study Psalm 51 KJV)
- Ask God for new mercy every morning and His grace (the grace of God will see you through).
- Ask God to provide you with your daily bread- (your provision for today)
- Repent, ask the Lord to show your areas of repentance
- Pray for others who have Lupus, and it's okay if you don't know their names.

Example of Prayer

by Minister Debbie Hollins

Father, in Jesus' name, I ask you to forgive me of my sins, as I pray for individuals who have Lupus flare-ups. I ask you to forgive them of their sins. And to heal them from the crown of their heads down to the sole of their feet. Father, I pray they walk in Forgiveness, and they are quick to repent. I speak life into their world. I say they shall live and not die; they shall declare the works of the Lord. I declare they are: strong in the Lord and the power of your might. They will love themselves as You love them. I come against all of their confusion today. I say they will have peace in their body, their soul and spirit, and mind. They shall lay down in peace and raise up in peace. They will not lose their mind, that you, Lord, keep them in perfect peace because their mind is staying on You. I say, they are whole, they are well, they are strong in You and their entire body today. I declare that heaven and earth agree with me today. Today Father, in Jesus' name, I claim them for you. I thank You, you are their wonder, you are everything they need. I thank You, You are moving for them, I thank You they will experience you today in more than one way. Thank You, Lord, in Jesus' name. Amen

- Pray for others; what you make happen for others, God will make happen for you.
- Be faithful in your reading, meditation, and studying of the Word of God
- Ask God to prepare someone who can support you
- Find you a church home

Finding Your Spiritual Church Home

Beloved, I wish above all things that thou mayest prosper and be in health, even as thy soul prospereth (3 John 2 King James Version).

If you can, go to church! Go to a church where they teach and preach the Word of God. Your church place helps feed you spiritually. Let me help you; do you see Jesus through your pastor? Is he or she preaching and teaching the Word of God? Can you sense God's presence there? Any demonstration of the Holy Spirit there? Are you learning more about the Word of God, and has it changed you some? Does it cause you to want more of the Word of God? What is God speaking to your heart about that place? God will definitely confirm your place of Worship to you.

> Please don't go where there is no life of God in the church; you need to be richly in the Word of God. Constantly feed your spirit the Word of God, grow daily in the Word of God. If God advises you to have your church lay hands, follow through with God order, but stay in the Word and don't quit because you are in a church. From this point on, the church is essential. Choose to follow the Word, to do the Word, and to become the Word. If you cannot go to church because of your sickness, use the same guidance going to the church above for

virtual church, there is no excuse, be the church and when you go, you know what to look for.

Walking your way through your spiritual journey. Understand, you must become the Word. You need to be filled with his Word, this will take time. God works through a yielded vessel, and he would like to work through yours. Remember, your salvation wasn't just for you. God needed workers in his vineyard to bring others into his kingdom. Learn God's ways. My old ways, old habits had to be transformed. God was working out his purpose for my life and was using this situation to prepare me for the future, destiny, and purpose. Could you imagine God had more outstanding, excellent, brilliant plans for my life than what I could imagine? Remember, reading is one way of learning about Jesus, but when you can meditate, you become one with the Word and then turn around and speak that same Word back unto God and then pray that Word with a heart of gratitude moves God.

My mediation in God's Words keeps me strong. The more I meditate, the more I eat the words. When I eat the Word, I am strong. I can endure. My mediation is the energy for my spirit, mind, body, and soul. My mediation causes me to grow spiritually, causes me to grow more in Christ Jesus because I increase my knowledge of Him. This is how you walk your way through your healing, the Word of God is life, for our soul, causes our spirit to become one with his spirit, it strengthens, provides, peace, joy, love, understanding. Follow Holy Spirit leading and guidance and stay on your medicine, just add your spiritual medicine which is the Word of God. Pray over your meds, hold them up before the Lord. I began to offer up the meds in thanksgiving.

Example of praying Over Meds

by Minister Debbie Hollins

Father in the name of Jesus I offer up these meds unto you now. I thank you for these meds will not in any means harm me. Your word said if we take up any deadly things it shall not hurt me. I thank You for keeping all side effects, mood swings, hallucination, nausea, the taste of meds, and other symptoms away from me. I thank you, I will be in my right mind, and it's mine for the asking. I believe therefore I received. None of this drug shall form against me shall hurt me, physically, mentally, emotionally, or spiritually. They will do what they are supposed to do, without any harm, in Jesus name, Amen

Let's Get Started

This Book of the Law shall not depart from your mouth, but you shall meditate in it day and night, that you may observe to do according to all that is written in it. For then you will make your way prosperous, and then you will have good success (Joshua 1:8 New King James Version).

Create a good study environment: Ask the Holy Spirit of God to come in and help teach you God's Word. You have not because you don't ask of him. (You are the student, and the Holy Spirit is the teacher). You can play, worship music, then come in, sit awhile and say Holy Spirit, I'm ready, teach me the things of the Father. Make sure you have all your study tools before you begin. Remember you in the presence of a gentleman.

Study Tools

- The Bible
- Dictionary, Bible Dictionary, Concordance (All of these online)

- Pen, pencil, highlighters, and paper
- Keep you a spiritual journal
- Write down whatever God shows you, what God is saying
- Index cards to write your scriptures on, post them where you visit the place the most.
- Guard your mind and spirit and heart by not watching things that are not good

Steps of Biblical Meditation on the Word of God
Step One: Search the healing scripture or other scriptures
Step Two: Find the one that stands out
Step Three: Write that scripture out
Step Four: Read the scriptures
Step Five: Meditate on the scriptures to help feed the inner man, strengthen your spirit, body, and soul.
Step Six: Once the Word of God is inside of you, use those exact words to stand on because they are now in you.
Step Seven: Your faith will grow; you need to hear the Word, see the Word, speak the Word, and the Word of God will grow richly within you.

God wants you clean, deliver, and whole:
"Wherever you are troubled in your spirit, find that particular Word and do the same as you did for healing. Don't believe the lies of the devil, know the truth, what is God's Word saying to you, in all thy getting understanding."

The Word of God

For the Word of God is living and active. Sharper than any double-edged sword, it penetrates even to dividing soul and spirit, joints and marrow; it judges the thoughts and attitudes of the heart (Hebrews 4:12 New International Version).

Prayer of Surrendering to God

by Minister Debbie Hollins

Father in Jesus' name, you are my source, my strength, my help in time of need, my prince of peace, the one who makes bitter experiences sweet, the One that is more than enough. Your word is a lamp to guide my feet and a light for my path. Thank You for being my strong tower, my rock, healer, and deliverer. I ask You to forgive me of all of my sins, I pray everyone whom I trespass against will forgive me of my trespasses and I stand to forgive them of their trespass against me. Father, I ask You to wash me, create in me a clean heart, O God, and renew a right spirit within me. I surrender my life unto you wholeheartedly, my desire is to always please you and to serve you. Teach me your ways. Father, I ask you to give me this day my daily bread. Thank you for providing everything for this day. Holy Spirit you lead and guide me in the areas I need to study for my life. Lord, help me not to sin against you, in Jesus name Amen.

Remember: *For I know the plans I have for you," declares the LORD, "plans to prosper you and not to harm you, plans to give you hope and a future (Jeremiah 29:11 NIV)*

Daily Biblical Meditation

"Let the words of my mouth,
and the meditation of my heart,
be acceptable in thy sight,
O LORD,
my strength,
and my redeemer.
(Psalm 19:14 KJV)

Growth is Vital

Jesus grew in wisdom and in stature and in favor with God and all the people (Luke 2:52 New Living Translations).

Walk in Obedience to God

Walk in obedience to all that the Lord your God has commanded you, so that you may live and prosper and prolong your days in the land that you will possess (Deuteronomy 5:33 New International Version).

Have Faith in God

And Jesus answering saith unto them, Have faith in God.

For verily I say unto you, That whosoever shall say unto this mountain, Be thou removed, and be thou cast into the sea; and shall not doubt in his heart, but shall believe that those things which he saith shall come to pass; he shall have whatsoever he said. Therefore I say unto you, when ye pray, believe that ye receive them, and ye shall have them. (Mark 11:22-24 King James version).

You didn't choose God, He chose You

You did not choose me, but I chose you and appointed you so that you might go and bear fruit- fruit that will last -and so that whatever you ask in my name the father will give you (New International Version).

Debbie Hollins

Keep On Asking and Receiving

And I say unto you, Ask, and it shall be given you; seek, and ye shall find; knock, and it shall be opened unto you. For every one that asketh receiveth; and he that seeketh findeth; and to him that knocketh it shall be opened. If a son shall ask bread of any of you that is a father, will he give him a stone? or if he ask a fish, will he for a fish give him a serpent? Or if he shall ask an egg, will he offer him a scorpion? If, yet then, being evil, know how to give good gifts unto your children: how much more shall your heavenly Father give the Holy Spirit to them that ask him? (Luke 11:9-13 King James Version)

Out of the Abundance of My Heart

A good man out of the good treasure of his heart brings forth good; and evil man out of the evil treasure of his heart brings forth evil. For out of the abundance of the heart his mouth speaks (Luke 6:45 New King James Version).

Confidence before God

Dear friends, if our hearts do not condemn us, we have confidence before God and receive from him anything we ask, because we keep his commands and do what pleases him (1 John 3:21-22 New International Version).

All Things Are Possible

But Jesus looked at them and said, "With men it is impossible, but not with God; for with God all things are possible (Mark 10:27 New King James Version).

The Prayers of the Righteous

Confess your faults one to another, and pray for one another, that ye may be healed. The effectual fervent prayer of a righteous man availeth much (James 5:16 King James version).

Death and Life

Death and life are in the power of the tongue: and they that love it and shall eat the fruit thereof (Proverbs 18:21 King James Version).

Humble Yourself

Humble yourselves in the sight of the Lord, and He will lift you up (James 4:10 New King James Version).

Words Accounts (watch Your Words)

But I say to you that for every idle word men may speak, they will give an account of it in the day of judgment. For by your words you will be justified, and by your words you will be condemned (Matthew 12:36-37 New King James Version).

First Greatest Commandment

Master, which is the greatest commandment in the law? Jesus said unto him, Thou shalt love the Lord thy God with all thy heart, and with all thy soul, and with all thy mind. This is the first and great commandment (Matthew 22: 36-38 King James Version).

Second Greatest Commandment

And the second is like unto it, Thou shalt love thy neighbour as thyself (Matthew 22:39 King James Version).

Love your enemies

But I say to you, love your enemies, bless them who curse you, do good to them that hate you, and pray for those who despitefully use you and persecute you; (Matthew 5:44 King James Version)

Cast Your Burden Upon the Lord

Cast your burden on the LORD, And He shall sustain you; He shall never permit the righteous to be moved (Psalm 55:22 New King James Bible)

Lay Up Treasure in Heaven

"Stop storing up treasures for yourselves on earth, where moths and rust destroy and thieves break in and steal. Instead, store up treasures for yourselves in heaven, where moths and rust don't destroy and thieves don't break in and steal. Your heart will be where your treasure is (Matthew 6: 19-21 King James Version).

God had not given us

For God has not given us a spirit of fear and timidity, but of power, love, and self-discipline (2 Timothy 1:7 New Living Translation)

All things were made

All things were made and came into existence through Him; and without Him not even one thing was made that has come into being. In Him was life [and the power to bestow life], and the life was the Light of men (John 1:3-4 Amplified Bible)

Let Your Light Shine

Let your light so shine before men, that they may see your good works, and glorify your Father which is in heaven (Matthew 5:16 King James Version).

Stand to Forgive

"And whenever you stand praying, If you have anything against anyone, forgive him, that your Father in heaven may also forgive you your trespasses. But, if you do not forgive, neither will your Father in heaven forgive your trespasses" (Mark 11:25-26 New King James version).

Calling Those Things in Being

(As it is written, I have made thee a father of many nations,) before him whom he believed, even God who quickeneth the dead, and calleth those things which be not as though they were (Romans 4:17 King James Version).

Walk by Faith

"(For we walk by faith, not by sight:)" (2 Corinthians 5:7 King James Version).

The Weapon of Our Warfare

(For the weapons of our warfare are not carnal but mighty through God to the pulling down strongholds;) Casting down imaginations, and every high thing that exalteth itself against the knowledge of God, bringing into captivity every thought to the obedience of Christ; And having in a readiness to revenge all disobedience is fulfilled. (2 Corinthians 10:4-6 King James Version)

Peace of God

And the peace of God, which passeth all understanding, shall keep your hearts and minds through Christ Jesus (Philippians 4:7 King James Version).

One Day With the Lord

But, beloved, be not ignorant of this one thing, that one day is with the Lord as a thousand years, and a thousand years as one day. The Lord is not slack concerning his promise, as some men count slackness; but is longsuffering to us-ward, not willing that any should perish, but that all should come to repentance (2 Peter 3:8-9 King James Version).

Healing Scriptures

Today I have given you the choice between life and death, between blessings and curses. Now I call on heaven and earth to witness the choice you made. Oh, that you and your descendants might live! (Deuteronomy 30:19 New Living Translation)

I shall not die, but live, and declare the works of the LORD (Psalm 118:17 King James Version)

Death and life are in the power of the tongue, And those who love it and indulge it will eat its fruit and bear the consequences of their words (Proverbs 18:21 Amplified Bible)

My son, pay attention to my words and be willing to learn; Open your ears to my saying. Do not let them escape from your sight; Keep them in the center of your heart. For they are life to those who find them, And healing and health to all their flesh. Watch over your heart with all diligence, For from it flow the springs of life (Proverbs 4:20-23 Amplified Bible).

For the life of the flesh is in the blood: and I have given it to you upon the altar to make an atonement for your souls: for it is the blood that maketh an atonement for the soul (Leviticus 17:11 King James Version).

Who his own self bare our sins in His own body on the tree, that we, being dead to sins, should live unto righteousness: by whose stripes ye were healed (1 Peter 2:24 King James Version).

He sent his word, and healed them, and delivered them from their destructions (Psalm 107:20 King James Version).

Surely he hath borne our griefs, and carried our sorrows: yet we did esteem him stricken, smitten of God, and afflicted. But he was wounded for our transgressions, but was bruised for our iniquities: the chastisement of our peace was upon him; and with his stripes we are healed (Isaiah 53:4-5 King James Version).

Bless the Lord, O my soul: and all that is within me, bless his holy name. Bless the Lord, O my soul, and forget not all his benefits: Who forgiveth all thine iniquities; who healeth all thy diseases; Who redeemeth thy life from destruction; who crowneth thee with lovingkindness and tender mercies; Who satisfieth thy mouth with good things; so that thy youth is renewed like the eagle's (Psalm 103: 1-5 King James Version).

Search the scripture there are a lot of scriptures on healing.

Your Assurance in God

And this is the confidence that we have in him, that, if we ask any thing according to his will, he heareth us: And if we know that he hear us, whatsoever we ask, we know that we have the petitions that we desired of him (1 John 5:14-15 King James Version).

God is not a man, that he should lie; neither the son of man, that he should repent: hath he said, and shall he not do it? Or hath he spoken, and shall he not make it good? (Numbers 23:19 King James Version)

I will lift up mine eyes unto the hills, from whence cometh my help. My help cometh from the Lord, which made heaven and earth (Psalm 121:1-2 King James Version).

Let us therefore come boldly unto the throne of grace, that we may obtain mercy, and find grace to help in time of need (Hebrews 4:16 King James Version).

Many are the afflictions of the righteous: but the LORD delivereth him out of them all (Psalm 34:19 King James Version).

"What do ye imagine against the LORD? He will make an utter end: affection shall not rise up the second time" (Nahum 1:9 King James Version).

For I am the Lord, I change not; therefore ye sons of Jacobs are not consumed (Malachi 3:6 King James Version).

Jesus Christ the same yesterday and today, and forever (Hebrews 13:8 King James Version).

For all the promises of God in him are yea, and in him Amen, unto the glory of God by us (2 Corinthians 1:20 King James Version).

And Jesus Healed Them All

I nstruction: Read one story daily. After you receive a clear understanding of the story, write out your takeaways in your journal. Then move on to the next one. Each of these stories enhances your faith. (Mark 1:32- 34 New King James Version), At evening, when the sun had set, they brought to Him all who were sick and those who were demon-possessed. And the whole city was gathered together at the door. Then He healed many who were sick with various diseases, and cast out many demons; and He did not allow the demons to speak, because they knew Him. All stories from King James Version.

Man with Infirmity for 38 years	John 5: 4-15 Healed
Man with Leper	Matthew 8:1-4 Healed
Man with Withered Hands	Matthew 12: 10-13 Healed
Woman with Issue of Blood for 12 years	Mark 5:25-34, Healed
Woman with Great Fever	Luke 4: 38 -39 Healed

| The man who was Unable to Speak | Matthew 9: 32 -34 Healed |
| Jesus raised Jairus Daughter | Mark 5: 21 -24, 35-43; Healed |

Jesus Christ is the same yesterday, and today and forever (Hebrews 13:8 New King James Version).

Prayer for Release

Evangelist Robert Hollins

Father in the Name of Jesus release all those which are bound by the enemy with any kind of sickness and disease. Oh Father release your love, that same love that the father has for his only begotten Son. Thank you Jesus for this special healing that you are releasing right now, heal and set free. Father, your special power is released in Jesus' Name. Jesus you are my deliverer, You are my healer, Father I give my sickness and disease to You Lord. You are my Lord. You are my love I am delivered and set free thank You for healing me In the Matchless Name of Jesus. Amen! Amen!

Salvation Assurances

Salvation is a free gift to anyone that hasn't received Jesus as Lord and Savior. In order to join the family of God, you must be born of the Spirit of God. There is no exception to the Kingdom of God. You must be born-again spiritual. Acts 2:21 King James Version, And it shall come to pass that whosoever shall call on the name of the Lord shall be saved. In Romans 10: 9-10 King James Version, That if thou shalt confess with thy mouth that the Lord Jesus and shalt believe in thine heart that God hath raised him from the dead, thou shalt be saved. For with the heart man believeth unto righteousness; and with the mouth confession is made unto salvation.

In order to be saved, you have to believe and open up your mouth to make the confession as stated above. After you receive Jesus as Lord, take the next step to receive the Baptism of the Holy Spirit. In Luke 11:13 King James Version, If ye then being evil, know how to give good gifts unto your children: how much more shall your heavenly Father give the Holy Spirit to them that ask him. Wow! That's good news. God the Father wants to give unto you himself completely. You don't have to be afraid to speak in tongues. Remember whatever words you are hearing, praise God and release them, God is waiting to fill you.

Prayer for Salvation and Baptism of the Holy Spirit

Evangelist Robert Hollins

All those who don't know the Lord and want to know the Lord and want to know him, say this ("Lord I'm a sinner and want to know You in a special way. My life has been up and down and I'm asking to be free and set free from the things that keep me from knowing You in the fullness. I confess right now of all my sins which I have committed. Lord, I believe you died and rose again for my sins. I'm willing to follow You today Lord. I invite You in Lord set me free now in Jesus Name") Thank You, Lord.

Now, Lord, I am asking you to fill me with your precious Holy Spirit. God empower me with your spirit and love. My desire for the presence of the Holy Spirit to engulf me to His glorious power, it's Not by might, nor, by power, but by my spirit, saith the Lord of hosts. Began to praise God for the utterance of speaking in tongues. We believe the evidence of speaking in tongues to be manifested now In Jesus Matchless Name. Amen and Amen.

Glossary

"Admirable." Merriam-Webster.com Dictionary, Merriam-Webster,
http://merriam-webster.com/dictionary/admirable.

"Affliction." Merriam-Webster1828 Dictionary
http://www.merriam-webster.com/dictionary/affliction.

"Inhabits." Merriam-Webster.com Dictionary, Merriam-Webster,
http://merriam-webster.com/dictionary/inhabits.

"Thing." Merriam-Webster.com Dictionary, Merriam-Webster,
http://merriam-webster.com/dictionary/thing.

Updated Resources

Lupus-Symptoms and Causes-Mayo Clinic Jan. 27, 2021
http://www.mayoclinc.org>lupus

What is Lupus? Oct. 21, 2020
http://www.lupus.org

Systemic Lupus Erythematosus (SLE) / CDC
http://www.cdc.gov>facts>details

Epilogue

In dealing with Lupus, everyone has a story. Everyone's journey, however, is not the same, but everyone who has Lupus in common can be saved, healed, whole, and delivered. I challenge you to find your place by stop letting Lupus control you. Turn it all around and you control it. Remember the doctors already gave you their reports which say, there is no cure. Don't let Lupus have you; you have it, but whatever you do; you need Jesus.

You need to walk into forgiveness of yourself, God, and others who dealt with you the wrong way. Be quick to forgive, stay in the word of God daily, study, meditate, act on the word, pray, and you will find yourself walking through your healing. How long? Between you and God.

Jesus is your waymaker, your source, your strength, your healer. The Holy Spirit is your leader, guide, counselor, and teacher. Come within the bed of affliction, your pain, your mourns, your groans, your hurt, your shame, your heartaches, your heartbreaks, your agonize, your anguish, your deep depression, your disappointment, your loneliness. Come within your place of despair, your place of emptiness, your favorite place of silence, your anger, your fog, your confusion, your unbelief, your mistrust, your worry, your burden. Come within your disobedience, your rebellious, and come within your wounds and live your life pleasing to God and yourself. Will you make the decision to accept the Lord Jesus and follow him today? Come on from Living Within the Confinements of Lupus.

Printed in the United States
by Baker & Taylor Publisher Services